Turbo Graphix Toolbox

version 1

Owner's Handbook

John Smith March 1961

TABLE OF CONTENTS

LIST OF FIGURES

INTRODUCTION

Welcome to the Turbo Graphix Toolbox. The procedures and functions that make up this software package will expand your repertoire of Turbo Pascal programming tools. With the aid of the Graphix Toolbox, you can develop high-resolution monochrome graphics for IBM PC and PC-compatible computers (using either an IBM or Hercules graphics card), and the Zenith Z-100 computer.

This manual makes extensive use of Turbo Pascal programming examples; a good working knowledge of Turbo Pascal is assumed. If you need to brush up on your Pascal knowledge, refer to the *Turbo Pascal* manual, and/or the *Turbo Tutor*.

What Can You Do With the Graphix Toolbox?

The Turbo Graphix Toolbox is a versatile package, designed for both simple and complicated graphics applications. Simple procedures allow you to draw

- Points

- Lines

- Rectangles with optional shading

- Ellipses

- Circles

High-level procedures let you create the more complex graphics that are often needed in business and scientific applications:

- Labeled pie charts

- Bar charts with programmable shading

- A variety of curves, using different linestyles and with optional smoothing

- Curve fitting

- Line and solid modeling

- Labeled coordinate axes

- Polygons of any shape, with optional rotation or translation

All your drawings can be displayed either on the full screen, or in windows that you define. You can also draw on a RAM (virtual) screen in memory, without display, and move the resulting images to the displayed screen when desired.

Here are some examples of the kind of drawings you'll soon be able to generate with the Graphix Toolbox.

Figure 0-1: A Sampler of Drawings Done with the Graphix Toolbox

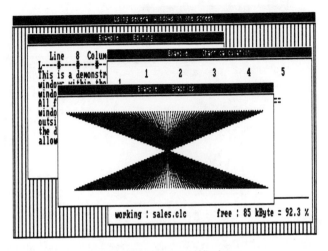

Figure 0-2: Stacked Windows

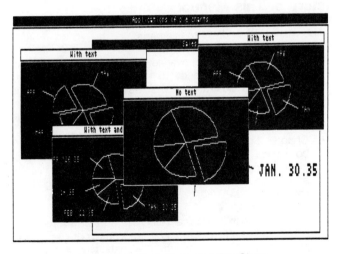

Figure 0-3: Variations on a Pie Chart

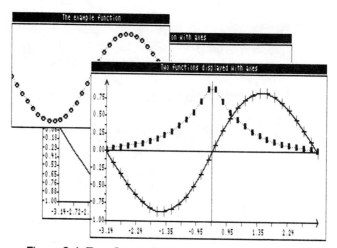

Figure 0-4: Two Curves Displayed with Coordinate Axes

Structure of This Manual

This manual is divided into five parts:

- Chapter 1 provides an overview of the Turbo Graphix Toolbox. Basic graphics terms you need to know in order to use the toolbox are defined, and illustrations of some of the things you can draw are given. This chapter also talks about the different hardware configurations that can run the Turbo Graphix Toolbox.

- Chapter 2 gets you started on using the Turbo Graphix Toolbox. Turbo Pascal examples for the most commonly used procedures are given, along with the resulting drawings. You'll also see how to define and manipulate windows, and save and print the graphic images you create.

- Chapter 3 is the technical reference part of the manual. All the constants, types, procedures, and functions contained in the Turbo Graphix Toolbox are described, in alphabetical order, with parameters, function, restrictions, and examples.

- Appendix A explains how to use the Turbo Graphix Toolbox with different hardware configurations.

- Appendix B provides a glossary of terms used in the manual.

Typography

The body of this manual is printed in normal typeface. Special characters are used for the following special purposes:

Alternate   Alternate characters are used in program examples and procedure and function declarations.

Italics   *Italics are used to emphasize certain concepts and terminology, such as predefined standard identifiers, parameters, and other syntax elements.*

Boldface   **Boldface type is used to mark reserved words, in the text as well as in program examples.**

Refer to the *Turbo Pascal Reference Manual* for a complete description of the syntax, special characters, and overall appearance of the Turbo Pascal language.

The Distribution Diskette

The Turbo Graphix Toolbox distribution diskette contains the following:

- Installation and demonstration files

- Files containing all the procedures and functions

- All the commented program examples used in Chapter 2

See the READ.ME! file for a complete list of all 53 files on your diskette. The distribution diskette is your only source for the Turbo Graphix Toolbox files. The first thing you should do upon receiving the diskette is to complete and mail the License Agreement at the front of this manual. You should then make a copy of the distribution diskette. Put the original diskette in a safe place, and use only the copy for doing your work. You should never use the distribution diskette for your work, since there is a charge for a replacement copy.

Acknowledgments

In this manual, references are made to several products:

- Flight Simulator is a registered trademark of Sublogic Inc.

- Hercules is a registered trademark of Hercules Computer Technology, Inc.

- IBM is a registered trademark of International Business Machines Inc.

- MS-DOS is a registered trademark of Microsoft Inc.

- Turbo Pascal is a registered trademark of Borland International Inc.

- Zenith Z-100 is a registered trademark of Heath Co.

Chapter 1
A COMPUTER GRAPHICS PRIMER

Before you do any drawing with the Turbo Graphix Toolbox, you will need to understand the graphics and screen display terms used throughout this manual. Each of these concepts is described below, followed by a list of the Turbo Graphix procedures and functions that apply to each.

Pixels

The term *pixel* is an acronym for *picture element*. Pixels, in fact, are the basic elements that make up a video display image. The tiny dots that combine to make the text and graphic images you see on your computer monitor are pixels.

The Turbo Graphix Toolbox allows you to display pixels as black or white with monochrome cards, or in any color supported by a color card.

Screens

A *screen* is the configuration of pixels that make up displayed text or graphic images. Depending on the type of graphics card installed in your system, the screen display will be made up of the following horizontal-by-vertical pixel dimensions:

- IBM 640x200

- Hercules 720x350

- Zenith 640x225

Because the Hercules display is made up of a greater number of pixels, the graphic images created are finer in grain—that is, they are higher in *resolution*. Because of their higher resolution, they also take longer to draw. IBM and Zenith graphics images are coarser grained, and therefore lower in resolution. The concept of resolution is easy to understand if you think of drawings made with pencils or pens; a drawing done with a fine-point drawing pen will be of a higher resolution, and will take longer to draw than one done with a blunt pencil.

For standard text display—that is, the text normally displayed by your system—a screen can also be thought of as a sequence of 80 vertical character columns that make up the width, and 25 lines of characters that make up the height.

There are two types of screens that you can use for creating images with the Toolbox: the screen displayed on your monitor, and a RAM (virtual) screen in memory. You can draw on either screen, but only the monitor screen is viewable; the RAM screen is invisible. The screen you are currently drawing on is called the *active screen*. RAM screens are useful for storing complicated images that are used often and are time consuming to redraw, or for animation, when it would be distracting to allow the computer to visibly redraw the screen.

The procedures and functions that are used to manipulate screens are:

ClearScreen	LoadScreen
CopyScreen	SaveScreen
GetScreen	SelectScreen
InvertScreen	SwapScreen

Characters and Fonts

A *character* is a letter, number, or symbol that is represented on your screen by a rectangular configuration of pixels. A sequence of characters makes up a display of *text*.

There are two styles—or *fonts*—in which text can be displayed with the Turbo Graphix Toolbox:

- A simple, 4x6-pixel upper- and lower-case font that is used to display window headers, pie chart labels, or any text you wish to display in integer multiples of 4x6 pixels

- A larger, higher quality font (8x8 pixels with an IBM card, 9x14 pixels with the Hercules card, and 8x9 pixels with the Zenith card) that corresponds to the font normally used with the particular graphics card installed in your system

Exactly how the Turbo Graphix Toolbox utilizes these two fonts will become clear when you read the next section about coordinate systems.

The procedures and functions that affect text are:

DC	DrawTextW
DefineHeader	TextDown
DefineTextWindow	TextLeft
DisplayChar	TextRight
DrawAscii	TextUp
DrawText	

Coordinate Systems

A *coordinate system* is a method used to identify a location according to its position relative to horizontal and vertical axes. In mathematics, usually, and in Turbo Graphix Toolbox programming in particular, the horizontal axis is labeled X, and the vertical axis Y. The exact location of, for example, a point, is determined by the X and Y coordinates of that point—that is, its distance from the X and Y zero axes.

Coordinate systems are extremely important in graphics programming, since all screen positions for text and graphics must be specified using X and Y coordinates. There are two types of coordinate systems that you can choose when working with the Turbo Graphix Toolbox: absolute screen and world coordinate systems.

Absolute Screen Coordinate System

The *absolute screen coordinate system* refers to the entire monitor screen, and the actual character and pixel screen positions, for plotting text and graphics; coordinates [0,0] are in the upper left corner of the screen, with the *X* coordinates increasing to the right, and the *Y* coordinates increasing downward. As mentioned earlier, the screen can be regarded either as a configuration of pixels or as a series of 25 lines by 80 columns.

Text is handled in two ways. The simple, 4x6-pixel font used for window headers and footers can be plotted anywhere on the screen, and can be scaled to be any size that is an integer multiple of 4x6 pixels (for example, 8x12). The higher quality font is plotted according to 80x25 text column and line coordinates.

World Coordinate System

For most graphics, the absolute screen coordinate system will not easily translate to the application's numeric values. A *world coordinate system* is an arbitrary coordinate system that you specify to accommodate your particular application. The numbers you use in your world coordinate system can be (and usually are) completely unrelated to pixel coordinates. In Turbo Graphix Toolbox language, this is called *defining a world*.

A world coordinate system can be used to scale images so that they fit correctly into the windows you have defined. After you define the world for a given window, any images you subsequently draw will be automatically, proportionately scaled to fit the window.

The procedures and functions that affect worlds are:

DefineWorld   ResetWorlds
FindWorld   SelectWorld

Windows

A *window* is any area of the screen that you define as the drawing area. Several windows, containing different drawings and text, can be defined and then displayed simultaneously on the screen. Each window can be moved independently of the other windows, placed on top of other windows, and stored to, recalled from, or erased from memory. Windows can be stored and loaded individually or in groups to and from disk. Several windows can be stored in RAM, and quickly copied to and from the active screen. You can draw borders, incorporate high-quality text, and label your windows with headers or footers. The window you are currently drawing in is called the *active window*.

A window can be specified to be almost any size, from the whole screen to 1 vertical pixel by 8 horizontal pixels. You define a window area by specifying the *X* and *Y* coordinates of its upper left and lower right corners, with *Y* coordinates measured in 1-pixel units and *X* coordinates measured in 8-pixel units. These coordinates are called *window definition coordinates*. In window definition coordinates, the point [0,0] refers to the upper left corner of the screen.

Once you're working within a window, you can redefine its world coordinate system, thereby allowing multiple images to be displayed within one window, each with its own coordinate system. Coordinate axes, along with lettering, can be easily added to any drawing.

A special RAM memory area, the *window stack*, is set aside for temporary storage of windows. The stack comes in handy when you have several windows that you want to keep but don't want to display all at the same time. The stack is also used for storing windows that would otherwise be erased when another window is moved over them on the screen.

The procedures and functions that affect windows are:

ClearWindowStack	RedefineWindow	SetClippingOff
Clip	RemoveHeader	SetHeaderOn
Clipping	ResetWindows	SetHeaderOff
CopyWindow	ResetWindowStack	SetHeaderToTop
DefineHeader	RestoreWindow	SetHeaderToBottom
DefineWindow	SaveWindow	SetWindowModeOff
DefineWorld	SaveWindowStack	SetWindowModeOn
DrawBorder	SelectWindow	StoreWindow
GetWindow	SelectWorld	WindowSize
InvertWindow	SetBackground	WindowStackSize
LoadWindow	SetBackground8	WindowX
LoadWindowStack	SetClippingOn	WindowY

Clipping

The Turbo Graphix Toolbox allows you to "clip" images at window boundaries if you wish. This feature accomplishes several purposes:

- It relieves you from having to be exact when you're drawing in a window. The Toolbox does the nitty-gritty work of keeping your work within window boundaries.

- It lets you "zoom in" on some aspect of a drawing. For example, let's say you've defined your world coordinate system for a window. Once you're working in the window, you can redefine the world. When the image is drawn, the Turbo Graphix program will "zoom in" and "clip" any part of your drawing that falls outside the window with the new coordinate system.

- It protects program memory. Drawings that stray outside screen boundaries can encroach on other parts of memory, including parts of your application program.

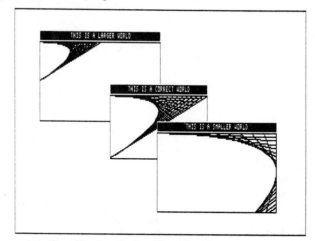

Figure 1-1: The Clipping Option Used To "Zoom In" on a Drawing

There are times when you'll choose not to clip drawings. For instance, you may develop a program using the clipping option, but once the program is debugged, and you know your drawings are within bounds, you can turn clipping off. This speeds up the drawing process considerably. Or, if you're working strictly with absolute coordinates, you don't need to worry about drawing outside screen boundaries.

How to Use the Turbo Graphix Toolbox With Your Hardware

There are a few differences between the computer systems and graphics cards that can run the Toolbox. In some cases, these differences require your special consideration when creating Toolbox-based programs.

There are two hardware considerations to take into account if you are using the IBM version of the the Turbo Graphix Toolbox: IBM compatibility, and graphics cards. The information below will tell you briefly what you need to know about your particular system; more technical details about certain hardware configurations can be found in Appendix A.

The IBM PC and True Compatibles

The Turbo Graphix Toolbox runs on any IBM PC, PC Jr., and compatible computer. But what exactly is a *true* IBM-compatible computer? There are many computers on the market today that are billed as IBM-compatible, and to some extent they are. However, when considering whether a computer is IBM compatible, it is important to look at the specific application you are using the computer for. In the case of the Turbo Graphix Toolbox, you must consider whether the graphics displayed by your computer will be true to your program design.

A potential problem with some IBM compatibles is that their screen display is of a higher resolution than the IBM screen. The Corona PC is a good example. Although the Corona's higher resolution display can make for very high-quality text and graphics, graphic images created with the Turbo Graphix Toolbox will not display true-to-form on the Corona screen; because of the Corona's higher resolution, the drawing will appear to be compressed vertically.

A good test for whether your IBM-compatible computer will run the Toolbox is to test the Flight Simulator program (written for the IBM PC) on your system. If your computer can run Flight Simulator, it's a good bet it will also run the Toolbox without problems.

Compatibility is also a consideration when your program will be running on more than one computer system. Some distortion of screen images may result when a program designed on a computer with an IBM card is run on a computer with a Hercules card. See Appendix A for information about how to cope with those kinds of problems.

Below is a list of computers and graphics cards that are sure to run the Turbo Graphix Toolbox. Next to the name of the product, the Turbo Graphix Toolbox version that runs with that product is given in parentheses. If your computer or graphics card is not on this list, give a call to Borland's technical support staff; they'll be able to tell you whether your computer will run the Graphix Toolbox.

AT&T PC 6300 (IBM)
Columbia MBC, VP (IBM)
Compaq Portable and DeskPro (IBM)
Comway Comgraphics card (Hercules)
Comway Comtronics (IBM)
Comway Comcolor (IBM)
Heath/Zenith Z100 series (Zenith)
Heath/Zenith Z150 series (IBM)
Hercules color card (IBM)
Hercules monochrome card (Hercules)
IBM Color/Graphics adapter (IBM)
IBM Enhanced Graphics adapter (IBM)
IBM PCjr (IBM)
Leading Edge PC (IBM)
MA Systems PC Peacock (IBM)
Panasonic SR Partner (IBM)
Paradise/USI MultiDisplay (IBM)
Paradise Modular Graphics Card (IBM)
Profit Systems Multigraph (IBM)
QuadRAM QuadColor I,II (IBM)
Seequa Chameleon line (IBM)
STB Graphics Plus II (IBM)
Tandy 1000 (IBM)
Tava (IBM)
Tecmar Graphics Master (IBM)
TeleVideo PC (IBM)
Tseng Laboratories UltraPAK (Hercules)
Vutek Color Plus (IBM)

IBM Color Graphics Card

If you have an IBM graphics card installed in your computer, your screen display is 640 pixels wide by 200 pixels tall. The *SetBackground-Color* and *SetForegroundColor* procedures are used to determine background and display image colors. You can also use the *SetColorWhite* and *SetColorBlack* procedures to reverse the background and foreground colors.

Hercules Monochrome Graphics Card

The Hercules graphics card produces a higher resolution display: 720 pixels wide by 350 pixels tall. The background of the display will be black, and the displayed images will be in the color produced by your monochrome monitor.

There are some important considerations to keep in mind when you decide to run your programs developed with a Hercules card on other systems. These and other potential problems are discussed in Appendix A.

Heath/Zenith Z-100 Computer

The Zenith version of the Turbo Graphix Toolbox produces a screen display 640 pixels wide by 225 pixels tall. The Z-100 computer runs the Turbo Graphix Toolbox in essentially the same way as an IBM-compatible computer. However, you have only seven colors to choose from when setting the color of the displayed images, and background color must be black.

Notes:

Chapter 2
GETTING STARTED

Ready to start drawing? This tutorial chapter takes you on a step-by-step tour of the Turbo Graphix Toolbox, using commented program examples for both basic and sophisticated graphics routines. The examples build on each other, so if you read the chapter through in order, by the end you should be ready to incorporate the Turbo Graphix routines you need into any graphics application program.

This chapter is designed as a basic tutorial. Technical details about the Turbo Graphix procedures used in this chapter can be found in Chapter 3. Basic graphics concepts and terminology used in this chapter are explained in Chapter 1 and Appendix B.

Including Turbo Graphix Routines in Your Program

To use the Turbo Graphix Toolbox, you must first incorporate three basic system files in your program with the Turbo Pascal *include directive*. The include directive is a comment that tells the compiler to read the program contained in the specified file. This directive starts with *$I*, followed by the file name and extension of the file to be included. To be understood by the Turbo Graphix Toolbox, the entire include directive must be enclosed within braces, i.e., *{$I filename.???}*. You must enter the include directive in the first column of your program text, before any code that utilizes the routines in the include file. Drive designations are also supported, and with Turbo 3.0, you can use full MS-DOS tree-structured directory path names.

Every Turbo Graphix program must include the following three system files, in the order given below.

```
{$I TYPEDEF.SYS}
{$I GRAPHIX.SYS}
{$I KERNEL.SYS}
```

You must copy the GRAPHIX file written for your hardware (supplied on the distribution disk) onto the GRAPHIX.SYS file. This is done by invoking the Turbo Graphix batch program, i.e., type *tginst hgc* or *tginst ibm*. Failure to do so may cause malfunctioning of your Turbo Graphix programs.

Next, before calling the Turbo Graphix routines you need for your particular application, you must initialize the graphics system by calling the *InitGraphic* procedure. At the end of your program, you must call *LeaveGraphic* to return your system to text mode. See Chapter 3 for detailed information about these procedures.

All of the example programs in this chapter are included on the Turbo Graphix Toolbox distribution disk, so you can try out the examples and experiment with the calling parameters in the various procedures. Each example program is listed under a file name of the form FILENAME.PAS.

Every program example consists of five basic steps:

•   Include at least the three core Turbo Graphix files

•   Call *InitGraphic* to enter graphics mode

•   Call *DrawBorder* to draw a border around the drawing area (optional)

•   Draw your images or text

•   Include a wait loop so you can view the display (optional)

•   Call *LeaveGraphic* to return to text mode

Drawing Points

You can use the Turbo Graphix *DrawPoint* procedure to draw points using either absolute screen or world coordinates. (See Chapter 1 for a definition of coordinate systems). The next two sections show you how to draw points using the screen coordinate system, while the section following explains how points are drawn in world coordinates. You should read this section even if you aren't interested in drawing points, because the rest of the examples in this chapter utilize world coordinate systems; it is important that you understand the point-drawing examples in order to see the difference between screen and world coordinate systems.

Drawing a Single Point

Writing a program that draws a single point is the simplest thing you can do with the Turbo Graphix Toolbox. Below is a Turbo Pascal program (DRWPNT.PAS on the distribution disk) that draws and displays a single point.

```
program ExamplePoint;

{$I typedef.sys}        {include system independent type definitions}
{$I graphix.sys}        {include system dependent defs and routines}
{$I kernel.sys}         {include system independent support routines}

begin

    InitGraphic;            {initialize the graphics system}
    DrawBorder;

    DrawPoint(100,100);     {draw the point}

    repeat until KeyPressed; {wait until a key is pressed}
    LeaveGraphic;           {leave the graphics system}

end.
```

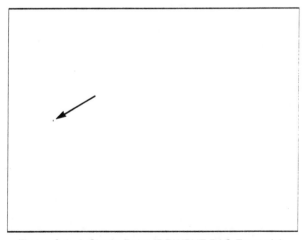

Figure 2-1: A Single Point (DRWPNT.PAS Example)

Drawing a Cluster of Points

The following program (DRWPNTS.PAS on the distribution disk) draws 1000 points, displayed randomly on the screen. For this example, let's assume you have an IBM graphics card installed in your system.

```
program DrawPoints;

{$I typedef.sys}              {include the graphics system code}
{$I graphix.sys}
{$I kernel.sys}

var i:integer;

begin
    InitGraphic;              {init the system and screen}
    DrawBorder;

    for i:=1 to 1000 do       {draw 1000 random points on IBM screen}
      DrawPoint(random(639),random(199));

    repeat until KeyPressed;  {wait until a key is pressed}
    LeaveGraphic;
end.
```

Figure 2-2: A Cluster of Points (DRWPNTS.PAS Example)

If you were to run this program on a system with a Hercules graphics card, the points would be drawn in the upper left corner of the screen. This is because the points are drawn in absolute screen coordinates. Since screen dimensions produced by the Hercules card are larger than IBM (720x350 instead of 640X200), and since coordinates [0,0] are in the upper left corner of the screen, the random points would be drawn as though they were on an IBM screen placed in the upper left corner of the Hercules screen.

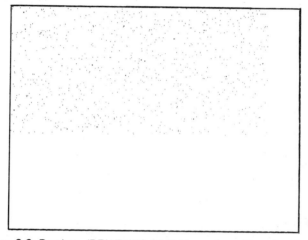

Figure 2-3: Previous (DRWPNTS.PAS) Example on Hercules Screen

To avoid this skewed placement, and to allow you to run your program on systems with different graphics cards, you can write this program so that it uses a world coordinate system instead of the absolute screen coordinate system, as described next.

Drawing Points Using a World Coordinate System

A *world coordinate system* lets you define the addressing dimensions of your drawing area, independently of the screen type and size. Once you have defined your world, the Turbo Graphix program will scale the drawing to fit the screen or window you are using.

The following program (WDRWPNTS.PAS on the distribution disk) is identical to the one in the previous section, but uses a world coordinate system instead of the absolute screen coordinate system.

```
program WorldDrawPoints;

{$I typedef.sys}                    {include the graphics system code}
{$I graphix.sys}
{$I kernel.sys}

var i:integer;

begin
   InitGraphic;                     {init the system and screen}
   DrawBorder;

   DefineWorld(1,0,1000,1000,0);    {define a world for drawing}
   SelectWorld(1);                  {select it}
   SelectWindow(1);

   for i:=1 to 1000 do              {draw 1000 random points on world}
      DrawPoint(random(1000),random(1000));

   repeat until KeyPressed;         {wait until a key is pressed}
   LeaveGraphic;
end.
```

Erasing a Point

To erase a point, change the drawing color to black, and then draw the point, as follows:

```
SetColorBlack;
DrawPoint(x,y);
```

Summary of Point Routines

DrawPoint draws a point in world or screen coordinates

DP draws a point in absolute screen coordinates only

PD returns TRUE if a point is drawn at specified screen coordinates

PointDrawn returns TRUE if a point is drawn at specified world coordinates

Drawing Lines

The *DrawLine* procedure allows you to draw and display lines in the current line style (selected by the *SetLineStyle* procedure). The coordinates for lines drawn in the following program examples are all calculated using world coordinate systems.

Drawing a Single Line

The following program (DRWLIN.PAS on the distribution disk) draws a line from the upper right to the lower left corner of the screen. Endpoint coordinates are passed to the procedure as the *X* and *Y* coordinates of the first endpoint, followed by the *X* and *Y* coordinates of the second endpoint.

```
program DrawLine;

{$I typedef.sys}              {include graphics system}
{$I graphix.sys}
{$I kernel.sys}

var i:integer;

begin
   InitGraphic;              {initialize the graphics system}
   DrawBorder;

   DefineWorld(1,0,1000,1000,0); {define the world to draw in}
   SelectWorld(1);
   SelectWindow(1);

   DrawLine(0,1000,1000,0);   {draw the line}

   repeat until KeyPressed;   {wait until a key is pressed}
   LeaveGraphic;              {leave the graphics system}
end.
```

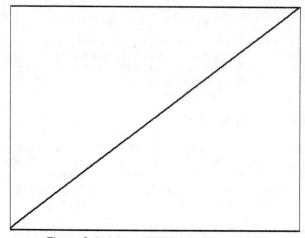

Figure 2-4: A Line (DRWLIN.PAS Example)

Drawing a "Walking Line"

An intriguing variation on the *DrawLine* procedure is the "walking line." A walking line program generates, by increments, a series of endpoint coordinates, thereby creating a "walking line." By changing the formula used to generate the endpoint coordinates, a variety of shapes can be drawn. In the example below (DRWLINS.PAS on the distribution disk), the first endpoint moves uniformly across the top of the screen from left to right, while the other endpoint moves incrementally and diagonally from the upper right to the lower left corner of the screen.

```
program DrawLines;

{$I typedef.sys}                {include the graphics system code}
{$I graphix.sys}
{$I kernel.sys}

var i:integer;

begin
  InitGraphic;                  {init the system and screen}

  DefineWorld(1,0,1000,1000,0); {define a world for drawing}
  SelectWorld(1);               {select it}
  SelectWindow(1);

  SetBackground(0);
  DrawBorder;

  for i:=1 to 20 do DrawLine(i*50,0,1000-i*50,i*50);

  repeat until KeyPressed;      {wait until a key is pressed}
  LeaveGraphic;
end.
```

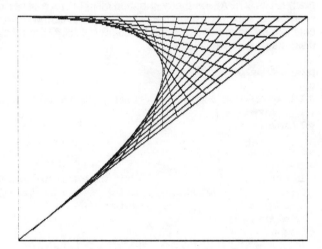

Figure 2-5: A Walking Line (DRWLINS.PAS Example)

Summary of Line-Drawing Routines

Clip clips a line at active window boundaries

DrawLine draws a line using world or screen coordinates

DrawLineClipped clips a line at screen boundaries

DrawStraight draws a horizontal line

SetLinestyle selects one of five linestyles for drawing lines

GetLinestyle returns the current linestyle

Drawing Squares

The *DrawSquare* procedure draws rectangles in the current line style (selected by the *SetLineStyle* procedure). A rectangle is defined by the coordinates of the points at its upper left and lower right corners. A boolean value, *Fill*, allows you to fill the rectangle with the current drawing color (determined by the *SetForegroundColor* procedure). The following program (DRWSQ.PAS on the distribution disk) draws a series of consecutively larger squares around the center of the screen, with no fill. Another example program not illustrated here (DRWHCH.PAS on the distribution disk) draws hatched squares.

```
program DrawSquares;

{$I typedef.sys}                    {include the graphics system code}
{$I graphix.sys}
{$I kernel.sys}


var i:integer;
begin
  InitGraphic;                      {init the system and screen}
  DefineWorld(1,0,1000,1000,0);     {define a world for drawing}
  SelectWorld(1);                   {select it}
  SelectWindow(1);
  DrawBorder;

  for i:=1 to 20 do DrawSquare(500-i*25,500-i*25,500+i*25,500+i*25,false);
  repeat until KeyPressed;          {wait until a key is pressed}
  LeaveGraphic;
end.
```

Figure 2-6: Squares (DRWSQ.PAS Example)

Summary of Square-Drawing Routines

DrawSquare draws a square using world coordinates

DrawSquareC draws a square using screen coordinates, but clipped at the boundaries of the active window

SetForegroundColor chooses the current drawing color

SetLinestyle chooses the line style

Drawing Circles

Because different graphics cards produce screen displays with different vertical-by-horizontal dimensions, and because different monitors have different screen proportions, a correctly-proportioned circle drawn on one screen may look distorted on another screen. To adjust for differences in screen proportions, Turbo Graphix routines that deal with circles and ellipses—*DrawCircle, DrawCircleSegment, DrawCartPie* and *DrawPolarPie*—utilize the concept of the *aspect ratio*.

An aspect ratio is defined as the height-to-width ratio of a circle or ellipse. Turbo Graphix circle routines allow you to vary the aspect ratio's vertical dimension by calling the *SetAspect* procedure. In addition, a global constant, *AspectFactor*, sets the system-dependent aspect ratio, so that an aspect ratio of 1.0 produces a true circle on a particular hardware screen.

The following program (DRWCIR.PAS on the distribution disk) draws a series of circles, and varies both their radii and aspect ratios. The parameters passed to the *DrawCircle* procedure specify the *X* and *Y* world coordinates of the center of the circle; the radius corresponds to the *X* (horizontal) dimension of the circle.

```
program DrawCirc;

{$I typedef.sys}              {include the graphics system code}
{$I graphix.sys}
{$I kernel.sys}

var i:integer;
    AspectLoc,rad:real;

begin
   InitGraphic;               {init the system and screen}
   DefineWorld(1,0,1000,1000,0);   {define a world for drawing}
   SelectWorld(1);            {select it}
   SelectWindow(1);
   DrawBorder;

   rad:=1.5;                  {set initial radius}
   AspectLoc:=GetAspect;      {save default aspect ratio}
   SetAspect(0.2);            {init it for this routine}

   for i:=1 to 15 do          {draw circles}
   begin
     DrawCircle(500,500,rad);
     SetAspect(0.2+i/10);
     rad:=rad-0.05;
   end;

   SetAspect(AspectLoc);      {restore previous aspect ratio}

   repeat until KeyPressed;   {wait until a key is pressed}
   LeaveGraphic;
end.
```

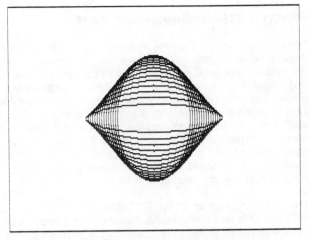

Figure 2-7: Circles (DRWCIR.PAS Example)

Summary of Related Routines

DrawCircle draws a circle or ellipse using world or screen coordinates

DrawCircleDirect draws a circle or ellipse using screen coordinates

DrawCircleSegment draws an arc of a circle

DrawPie draws a pie chart

GetAspect returns the current aspect ratio

SetAspect determines the aspect ratio for a circle

Text

As explained in Chapter 1, the Turbo Graphix Toolbox supports both a 4x6-pixel text and a machine-dependent text. The size of machine-dependent characters is 8x8 pixels for IBM, 9x14 pixels for Hercules, and 8x9 pixels for Zenith.

Displaying Machine-Dependent Text

The text routines used by the Turbo Graphix Toolbox are very similar to those used by Turbo Pascal; the screen is defined as 25 lines by 80 columns (characters), and the Turbo Pascal procedures *GotoXY, Write* and *WriteLN* are supported by the Graphix Toolbox. However, there are a few considerations specific to the Turbo Graphix text mode concerning the alignment of text with drawings, and within windows. Since the size of the text font varies with the graphics card installed, some adjustments must be made when attempting to align text with drawings. In particular, Hercules text, which is defined on a 9-pixel horizontal boundary, must be adjusted for the 8-pixel window boundary. See Appendix A for technical information on text fitting.

The following program (DRWSTXT.PAS on the distribution disk) places the start of a text string at the center of the screen, demonstrates the automatic new-line performed by *WriteLN*, and places the text within a filled box whose dimensions are determined according to the world coordinate system. The coordinates for the points at the corners of the box are computed from the character positions of the text.

```
program DrawStandardText;

{$I typedef.sys}                    {include graphics system}
{$I graphix.sys}
{$I kernel.sys}

const MaxWorldX: real=1000.0;
      MaxWorldY: real=1000.0;

var i:integer;
    CharHeight,CharWidth:real;

begin
  InitGraphic;                      {initialize the graphics system}

  DefineWorld(1,0,MaxWorldY,MaxWorldX,0);   {define world to draw in}
  SelectWorld(1);
  SelectWindow(1);
  DrawBorder;
```

```
GotoXY(39,12);                    {goto the center of the text screen}
writeln('* <- This should be at the center ');    {do two lines of text}
write('This should be on the next line');

CharWidth:=MaxWorldX/80;     {compute a character's width}
CharHeight:=MaxWorldY/25;    {compute a character's height}

DrawSquare(9*CharWidth,7*CharHeight,        {draw box at text loc [10,8]}
        (22*CharWidth)+2,(8*CharHeight)+2,true);

GotoXY(10,8);                     {write text in it}
write('Text in a box');

repeat until KeyPressed;          {wait until a key is pressed}
LeaveGraphic;                     {leave the graphics system}
end.
```

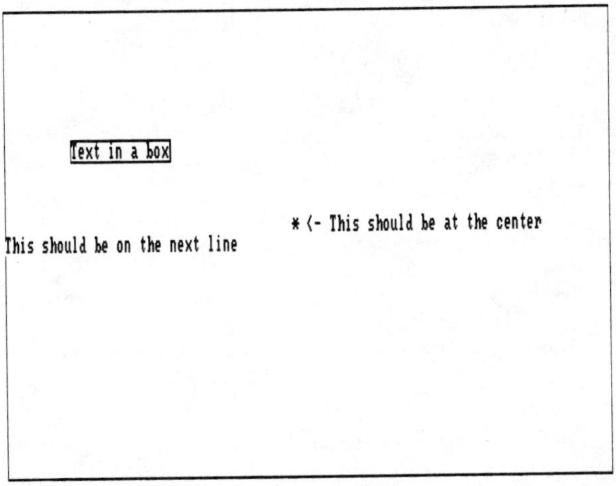

Figure 2-8: Machine-Dependent Text (DRWSTXT.PAS Example)

Displaying 4x6-Pixel Text

The 4x6-pixel character set is used for window headers, and for applications that require text that is smaller or larger than the machine-dependent text. Unlike the machine-dependent text, the 4x6-pixel characters can be placed at any screen location. The *Scale* parameter passed to the *DrawText* procedure specifies the size of the characters (in integer multiples of 4x6 pixels); the larger the value of *Scale*, the larger the character.

Since a character in the 4x6-pixel font is made up of only a few pixels, this text is of a coarser quality than the machine-dependent text, even when they are scaled to the same size.

The following example (DRWATXT.PAS on the distribution disk) uses the *DrawText* procedure to display upper-case characters, in different positions and sizes, in the center of the screen. The complete character set is then displayed at the upper left corner of the screen, scaled to its smallest size.

```
program DrawAlternateText;

{$I typedef.sys}                        {include graphics system}
{$I graphix.sys}
{$I kernel.sys}


const MaxWorldX: real=1000.0;
     MaxWorldY:  real=1000.0;
     CharArray1: array [0..25] of char=
       ('A','B','C','D','E','F','G','H','I','J','K','L',
        'M','N','O','P','Q','R','S','T','U','V','W','X','Y','Z');
                                        {define an array of characters}
var i:integer;
    CharHeight,CharWidth:real;

begin
  InitGraphic;                          {initialize the graphics system}

  DefineWorld(1,0,MaxWorldY,MaxWorldX,0);  {define the world to draw in}
  SelectWorld(1);
  SelectWindow(1);
  DrawBorder;
```

```
for  i:=1 to 50 do              {print random characters in center of screen}
    DrawTextW(random(600)+200,random(600)+200,
                 random(5),CharArray1[random(26)]);

DrawTextW(15,50,1,'ABCDEFGHIJKLMNOPQRSTUVWXYZ');    {type chars in corner}
DrawTextW(15,100,1,'abcdefghijklmnopqrstuvwxyz');
DrawTextW(15,150,1,'1234567890-=\' !@#$%^&*()_+|');
DrawTextW(15,200,1,'[]{}:";,.<>/?');

repeat until KeyPressed;              {wait until a key is pressed}
LeaveGraphic;                         {leave the graphics system}
end.
```

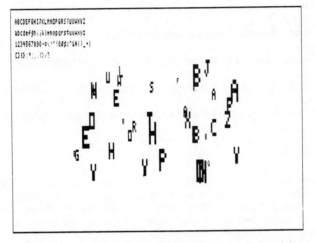

Figure 2-9: 4x6-Pixel Text (DRWATXT.PAS Example)

Summary of Text-Drawing Routines

For machine-dependent text:

DC draws a character at the specified text coordinates

DefineTextWindow uses specified text coordinates to define a window

DisplayChar draws a character at the specified text coordinates

TextDown, TextLeft, TextRight, TextUp adjust space between window boundaries and text (text fitting)

For 4x6-pixel text:

DefineHeader defines a window header

DrawAscii draws a character at the specified screen coordinates

DrawText draws a character string at the specified screen coordinates

DrawTextW draws a character string at the specified world coordinates

Windows

This section tells you how to create and manipulate on-screen windows. The use of windows allows greater flexibility in graphics applications, since you can display several different drawings on the screen at once, using different world coordinate systems; and you are not limited to the pixel dimensions of the window.

Defining a Window

When the Turbo Graphix Toolbox is initialized with the *InitGraphic* procedure, the entire screen is, in effect, defined as a window whose world coordinates correspond to the pixel dimensions of the screen. However, you can redefine any region of the screen as a window, from an 8x1-pixel (horizontal by vertical) box to the entire screen.

Once defined, a window acts more or less independently of other windows and even the screen. Windows can be small or large, moved around, drawn on with reference to their own coordinate systems and boundaries, and individually removed, stored, and retrieved.

Generally, you will want to define a new world coordinate system for every window you define; otherwise, any drawing you do in a window will take place as if the screen coordinate system were mapped to that window. All drawing routines—except routines internal to the graphics system, routines for machine-dependent text positioning such as *GotoXY*, and window positioning routines—can use world coordinate systems.

To associate a world with a window, you must always call *SelectWorld* before *SelectWindow*. If a new window is subsequently selected, the current world is retained. Thus, to draw alternately in two windows with different worlds, *SelectWorld* must be called before each *SelectWindow*:

```
repeat
  SelectWorld(1);
  SelectWindow(1);
    { Insert code to draw something in window 1
      using world coordinate system 1 }
  SelectWorld(4);
  SelectWindow(2);
    { Insert code to draw something in window 2
      using world coordinate system 4 }
until KeyPressed;
```

Besides simply defining the dimensions of your window, you can label it with a header or footer, fill it in with a color or background pattern, or draw a border around it in any line style. When a new window is defined or an existing window is redefined, the header associated with that window number is destroyed. This means that *DefineWindow* must be called before *DefineHeader*.

To change the dimensions of an existing window, without changing its header, use the *RedefineWindow* procedure.

The following example (SIMPWIND.PAS) shows you how to define a window with a border and a header.

```
program SimpleWindow;

{$I typedef.sys}          {these files must be}
{$I graphix.sys}          {included and in this order}
{$I kernel.sys}
{$I windows.sys}

begin
  InitGraphic;            {initialize the graphics system}
  DrawBorder;             {draw a border around the drawing}
                          {area of the primary window}
  DefineWindow(1,10,20,XMaxGlb-10,YMaxGlb-20); {define a window 80 pixels}
                          {in from the left and right edges, and 20}
                          {from the top and bottom edges}
  DefineHeader(1,'THIS IS AN EXAMPLE WINDOW'); {give it a header}
  SetHeaderOn;
  SetBackground(85);      {give it a grey background}
  SelectWindow(1);        {select the window}
  SelectWorld(1);         {select the world}
  DefineWorld(1,0,1000,1000,0); {give it a world coordinate system}
  DrawBorder;             {draw the border}
  repeat until KeyPressed; {wait until a key is pressed}
  LeaveGraphic;           {leave the graphics system}
end.
```

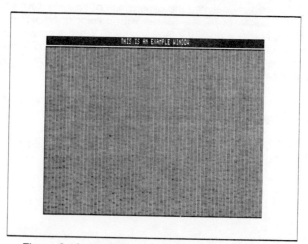

Figure 2-10: A Window (SIMPWIND.PAS Example)

Displaying a Drawing in a Window

Suppose you want to display the "walking line" example in a window. You can display the example using a world coordinate system, and in any position on the screen by following these steps:

- Define the window

- Define the world coordinate system for the window

- Select the world coordinate system

- Select the window for drawing

- Draw a border (optional)

- Display the walking lines

The following example (MULTWIND.PAS) displays the walking line example in three different windows, each with its own coordinate system, with the drawings clipped at window boundaries.

```
program MultipleWindows;

{$I typedef.sys}          {these files must be}
{$I graphix.sys}          {included and in this order}
{$I kernel.sys}
{$I windows.sys}

var i: integer;

procedure DrawLines;
var i:integer;
begin
  for i:=1 to 20 do DrawLine(i*50,0,1000-i*50,i*50);
end;
```

```
begin
  InitGraphic;                   {initialize the graphics system}
  DrawBorder;                    {draw a border around the drawing}
                                 {area of the primary window}
                                 {(the dimensions of the primary window}
                                 {default to the screen dimensions)}
  DefineWindow(1,trunc(XMaxGlb/10),trunc(YMaxGlb/10),
               trunc(XMaxGlb/2),trunc(YMaxGlb/2));
                                 {define a window  one tenth of the way}
                                 {in from the left and top edges, and half}
                                 {way down from the right and bottom edges}

  DefineHeader(1,'THIS IS A LARGER WORLD'); {give it a header}
  DefineWorld(1,0,2000,2000,0); {give it a larger world coord. system}
  DefineWindow(2,trunc(XMaxGlb/3),trunc(YMaxGlb/3),
               trunc((XMaxGlb*2)/3),trunc((YMaxGlb*2)/3));
                                 {define a window  one third of the way}
                                 {in from the left and top edges, and}
                                 {from the right and bottom edges}

  DefineHeader(2,'THIS IS A CORRECT WORLD'); {give it a header}
  DefineWorld(2,0,1000,1000,0); {give it a correct world coord. system}
  DefineWindow(3,trunc(XMaxGlb/2),trunc(YMaxGlb/2),
               trunc((XMaxGlb*9)/10),trunc((YMaxGlb*9)/10));
                                 {define a window  one half of the way}
                                 {in from the left and top edges, and half}
                                 {way down from the right and bottom edges}

  DefineHeader(3,'THIS IS A SMALLER WORLD'); {give it a header}
  DefineWorld(3,0,500,500,0); {give it a smaller world coordinate system}

  for i:=1 to 3 do
    begin
      SelectWorld(i);            {select it}
      SelectWindow(i);           {select it}
      SetHeaderOn;
      SetBackground(0);          {give it a black background}
      DrawBorder;                {draw border}
      DrawLines;                 {draw lines}
    end;

  repeat until KeyPressed;       {wait until a key is pressed}
  LeaveGraphic;                  {leave the graphics system}
end.
```

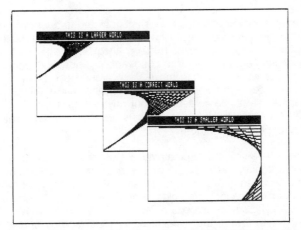

Figure 2-11: Three Windows (MULTWIND.PAS Example)

Moving Windows

Once you've defined a window, you can move it to any position on the screen using the *MoveVer* and *MoveHor* procedures; windows are moved by increments (multiples of 8 horizontal pixels and multiples of 1 vertical pixel).

MoveHor and *MoveVer* work by automatically and continually refreshing the screen images over which the window is moved. They do this by storing the displayed screen image to the virtual screen.

If you want to move multiple windows, things get a bit more complicated; you must manage the windows and other screen images yourself. What this means is that you must continually rebuild the virtual screen image every time you move windows. If there are any images on the screen that you wish to keep, you must copy those images either to the window stack with the *StoreWindow* procedure (if the images are in a window) or to the RAM (virtual) screen with the *CopyWindow* or *CopyScreen* procedure (if the images are on the screen) so they can be retrieved later; otherwise, when you move a window over those images, they will be erased, and there will be no way to restore them.

For your windows to keep their integrity and to be moved independently, you must keep copies of all windows on the window stack, and store all screen images you want to keep on disk. For instance, if the screen contains two windows that you want to display independently—that is, you want to be able to move them around and place them on top of each other—you should do the following: using the *SaveScreen* procedure, store the screen (without any windows) on disk, and store up-to-date copies of both windows on the window stack using the *StoreWindow* procedure.

Every time you draw something in a window, or change what was previously drawn, save a copy of the window on the window stack. When you want to move a window, save the presently displayed screen—without the window you plan to move—to the RAM virtual screen using the *CopyScreen* procedure, so the non-moving window is now also copied to the virtual screen. The virtual screen should now contain everything that was on the displayed screen, except the window you want to move. Now, draw the window you want to move on the screen, and use *MoveHor* and *MoveVer* to move the window around, without destroying the fixed images underneath.

The *window stack* is a RAM memory area where window images can be stored temporarily. You might want to use the stack when, for instance, you have defined and drawn in several windows but only want to display a few on the screen, or if one window is obstructing another and the obstructed window needs to be displayed. Whole window stacks, as well as individual windows in the stack, can be stored to and recalled from disk using the *SaveWindow* and *RestoreWindow* procedures. Windows on the stack can be accessed in any order.

Windows can be restored from the stack to any location on the screen by specifying *X* and *Y* offsets. To restore the window to its former position, use offsets of 0.

If the window currently selected with the *SelectWindow* procedure is the same as the one being restored from the stack, the screen coordinates of the selected window will shift to match the offset of the restored window. The selected window does *not* change when any other window is restored from the stack.

Stored windows and the RAM screen are dynamically allocated on the heap using the Turbo *GetMem* and *FreeMem* procedures. Therefore, the *Mark/Release* method of memory management should not be used in your programs.

The following program (MOVEWIND.PAS) shows how to move windows about on the screen; use the arrow keys to move the windows, and press the space bar to stop program execution.

```
program MoveWindows;

{$I typedef.sys}          {these files must be}
{$I graphix.sys}          {included and in this order}
{$I kernel.sys}
{$I windows.sys}

var i: integer;
    Ch: char;

procedure DrawLines;
var i:integer;
begin
  for i:=1 to 20 do DrawLine(i*50,0,1000-i*50,i*50);
end;

begin
  InitGraphic;                {initialize the graphics system}
  DrawBorder;                 {draw a border around the drawing}
                              {area of the primary window}
                              {(the dimensions of the primary window}
                              {defaults to the screen dimensions)}
  DefineWindow(1,trunc(XMaxGlb/10),trunc(YMaxGlb/10),
               trunc(XMaxGlb/2),trunc(YMaxGlb/2));
                              {define a window  one tenth of the way}
                              {in from left and top edges and half}
                              {way down from right and bottom edges}
  DefineHeader(1,'THIS IS THE FIXED WINDOW'); {give it a header}
  DefineWorld(1,0,1000,1000,0); {give it a world coordinate system}
  DefineWindow(2,trunc(XMaxGlb/2),trunc(YMaxGlb/2),
          trunc((XMaxGlb*9)/10),trunc((YMaxGlb*9)/10));
                              {define a window  one half of the way}
                              {in from left and top edges, and half}
                              {way down from right and bottom edges}
  DefineHeader(2,'THIS IS THE MOVEABLE WINDOW'); {give it a header}
  DefineWorld(2,0,1000,1000,0); {give it a world coordinate system}
  SelectWorld(1);             {select world}
  SelectWindow(1);            {select fixed window}
  SetHeaderOn;
  SetBackground(0);           {give it a black background}
```

```
DrawBorder;                    {draw the window}
DrawLines;                     {draw lines in it}
CopyScreen;                    {copy it to the virtual screen}
SetBreakOff;                   {don't error when edge hit}
SetMessageOff;
SelectWorld(2);                {select world}
SelectWindow(2);               {select moveable window}
SetHeaderOn;
SetBackground(0);              {give it a black background}
DrawBorder;                    {draw the window}
DrawLines;                     {draw lines in it}

repeat
  read(Kbd,Ch);                {read the keystroke}
  case ord(Ch) of
    72 : MoveVer(-4,true);     {up arrow?}
    75 : MoveHor(-1,true);     {left arrow?}
    77 : MoveHor(1,true);      {right arrow?}
    80 : MoveVer(4,true);      {down arrow?}
  end;
until Ch=' ';                  {space char exits program}

LeaveGraphic;                  {leave the graphics system}
end.
```

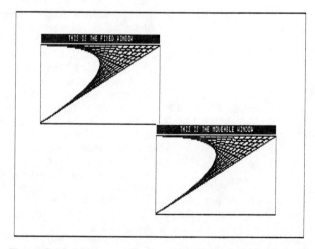

Figure 2-12: Moving a Window (MOVEWIND.PAS Example)

Another Use for Windows: the Flow Chart

Anything that can be contained in a rectangle can be animated using windows. The following example (FLOWDEMO.PAS) animates a flow chart by using a moveable window. The drawing of the flow chart is the fixed screen image, while a window that contains the present state of the "machine" is moved along the flow chart drawing to show how the processor modifies variables when the program executes. The program increments a count and tests the result. If the count is not large enough, the program increments the count and tests again. When the count is high enough, the "program" is finished.

```
program FlowDemo;

{$I typedef.sys}              {these files must be}
{$I graphix.sys}             {included and in this order}
{$I kernel.sys}
{$I windows.sys}

procedure FlowChartDemo;

var X1,Y1,X2,Y2,i,Count:integer;
    Temp:wrkstring;

  procedure DrawArrowHor(X1,Y1,X2,Y2:integer);  {draw horizontal arrow}
                                                 {with tip at point [X2,Y2]}
  begin
    DrawLine(X1,Y1,X2,Y2);
    if X2>X1 then
      begin
        DrawLine(X2-4,Y2-2,X2,Y2);
        DrawLine(X2-4,Y2+2,X2,Y2);
    end
      else
      begin
        DrawLine(X2+5,Y2-2,X2,Y2);
        DrawLine(X2+5,Y2+2,X2,Y2);
      end;
  end;
```

```
procedure DrawArrowVer(X1,Y1,X2,Y2:integer);  {draw vertical arrow}
                                              {with tip at point [X2,Y2]}
begin
  DrawLine(X1,Y1,X2,Y2);
  if Y2>Y1 then
   begin
    DrawLine(X2-2,Y2-3,X2,Y2);
    DrawLine(X2+2,Y2-3,X2,Y2);
   end
  else
   begin
    DrawLine(X2-2,Y2+3,X2,Y2);
    DrawLine(X2+2,Y2+3,X2,Y2);
   end;
end;

procedure Blink(Count,time:integer);    {blink the current window}
var i:integer;
begin for i:=1 to Count do
  begin
    Delay(time);
    InvertWindow;
  end;
end;

begin    {FlowChartDemo}
  DefineWindow(1,0,0,79,185);           {define the 'FLOW CHART'window}
  DefineWindow(2,12,20,25,40);          {define the 'START' window}
  DefineWindow(3,15,55,22,75);          {define the 'I=1' window}
  DefineWindow(4,11,110,26,130);        {define the 'IF I<=5' window}
  DefineWindow(5,47,90,56,110);         {define the 'I=I+1' window}

  ClearScreen;                          {draw the surrounding window}
  SetColorWhite;

  DefineHeader(1,'A FLOW CHART');
  SetHeaderOn;
  SelectWindow(1);
  DrawBorder;
  SetHeaderOff;
  SelectWindow(2);                      {draw the 'START' window}
  DrawBorder;
  DrawText(125,27,2,'START');
  SetWindowModeOff;
  DrawArrowVer(151,40,151,55);          {draw the connecting line}
  SetWindowModeOn;
```

```
SelectWindow(3);                       {draw the 'I=1' window}
DrawBorder;
DrawText(136,63,2,'I=1');
SetWindowModeOff;
DrawArrowVer(151,75,151,110);          {draw the connecting line}
SetWindowModeOn;
SelectWindow(4);                       {draw the 'IF I>=5' window}
DrawBorder;
DrawText(108,118,2,'IF I<=5');
DrawStraight(215,417,120);             {draw the connecting lines}
SetWindowModeOff;
DrawArrowVer(417,120,417,110);
DrawArrowVer(151,130,151,155);
SetWindowModeOn;
SelectWindow(1);
DrawText(300,110,2,'YES');
DrawText(160,137,2,'NO');

SelectWindow(5);                       {draw the 'I=I+1' window}
DrawBorder;
DrawText(390,98,2,'I=I+1');
SetWindowModeOff;
DrawLine(417,90,417,80);               {draw the connecting lines}
DrawArrowHor(417,80,151,80);

SetAspect(1.0);                        {draw the 'END' circle}
DrawCircle(151,165,25);
SelectWindow(1);
DrawText(137,163,2,'END');
SetWindowModeOn;
SetHeaderOn;

CopyScreen;                            {make an image of this screen}
                                       {on the virtual RAM screen}

{ClearEol(25);}
{gotoxy(27,25);}

DefineWindow(2,15,21,22,39);           {set up the moving window}
SelectWindow(2);
SetBackground(0);
DrawBorder;
InvertWindow;
Delay(1000);
```

```
InvertWindow;

Temp:='123456';                          {initialize the number array}
MoveVer(35,true);                        {move window over init statement}
DrawText(139,63,2,'I='+Temp[1]);         {'init' it}
Blink(30,50);
MoveVer(55,true);                        {move it down to increment loop}

for Count:=2 to 6 do                     {do increment loop}
    begin
      Delay(500);
      MoveHor(33,true);
      MoveVer(-20,true);
      SetBackground(0);
      DrawBorder;
      DrawText(400,98,2,'I='+Temp[Count]);
      Blink(30,50);
      MoveVer(-20,true);
      MoveHor(-33,true);
      MoveVer(40,true);
    end;

    InvertWindow;
    Delay(1000);
    MoveVer(46,true);                    {move to the 'END' statement}
    Blink(30,50);

    MoveHor(45,true);                    {move back up to the top}
    MoveVer(-136,true);
    MoveHor(-45,true);
    SetHeaderOn;
end;

begin
  InitGraphic;                           {initialize the graphics system}
  FlowChartDemo;                         {do the demo}
  repeat until KeyPressed;               {wait until a key is pressed}
  LeaveGraphic;                          {leave the graphics system}
end.
```

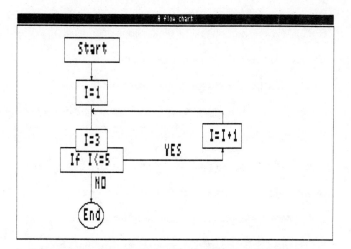

Figure 2-13: A Flow Chart (FLOWDEMO.PAS Example)

Summary of Window Routines

ClearWindowStack deletes a window from the stack

CopyScreen copies the active screen onto the inactive screen

CopyWindow copies a window from one screen to another

DefineHeader defines a window header

DefineWindow defines an area of the screen as a window

DefineWorld defines a world coordinate system

DrawBorder draws a line around the window

GetWindow returns the code number of the active window

InvertWindow inverts the color of the active window

LoadWindow loads a window from disk to the specified world coordinates

LoadWindowStack stores a window stack from disk to the window stack

RedefineWindow changes the dimensions of an existing window

RemoveHeader removes a window header

ResetWindowStack erases all windows from the stack

ResetWindows sets all windows to the size of the physical screen

SaveWindow saves a window to disk

SaveWindowStack saves a window stack to disk

SelectWindow selects a window for drawing

SelectWorld selects a world coordinate system

SetHeaderOff,SetHeaderOn determine whether a window header is displayed

SetHeaderToBottom, SetHeaderToTop place a header at the bottom or top of a window

SetWindowModeOff, SetWindowModeOn determine whether drawing takes place in a window or on the screen

Store Window stores a window on the window stack

WindowMode returns the window status

WindowSize determines whether there is room for a window on the stack

WindowStackSize returns the number of free bytes on the window stack

Pie and Bar Charts

Pie and bar charts provide a way to graphically represent numeric results that are common to many business and statistical applications. Three high-level routines—*DrawCartPie* and *DrawPolarPie* for pie charts, and *DrawHistogram* for bar charts—do most of the work required to display information in pie and bar charts; all you have to do is supply the numerical data. As long as you are familiar with Turbo Pascal, the program examples used in this section can be easily tailored to a particular application.

Pie Charts

Pie charts are used to display a series of values or percentages (the pie "slices") that make up a total unit (the whole pie). A pie chart shows, at a glance, the relative proportion of the whole that is represented by each value. For instance, a pie chart format is an effective way to show a company's market share, or the results of a scientific experiment.

The *DrawCartPie* and *DrawPolarPie* procedures not only automatically draw a pie chart that corresponds to your input values; they can also label each pie segment with text and/or a numeric value, as well as pull any pie segment away from the pie for display emphasis. Although pie charts can be drawn with reference to either world or screen coordinates, it is usually best to use world coordinates, especially if you want your program to run correctly on different computer systems. Also, pie charts drawn using a world coordinate system will be correctly proportioned in any given window, regardless of the size of the window.

A pie chart is drawn by passing the following parameters:

• Coordinates of the center point of the pie

• Coordinates of the starting point of the first pie segment

• Value and optional label of each segment in an array

• Desired labeling options

• Scale of the label characters (multiples of 4x6 pixels)

A pie chart can be specified so that the starting point of the first segment of the pie chart is referenced to either of two coordinate systems: Cartesian coordinates [X, Y], or polar coordinates [*Radius, Angle*]. The *Cartesian coordinate system*, used by the *DrawCartPie* procedure, allows the drawing to be referenced to a position located by [X, Y] coordinates. For instance, the first pie segment can be defined by a point relative to the center of the pie. The *polar coordinate system* references the pie chart to its radius and the angle of its first segment.

It is usually easiest to use polar coordinates—that is, to think of a pie chart as a circle with a certain radius, and with its first segment starting at a particular angle. The *DrawPolarPie* procedure uses polar coordinates. Since this is the method used most often, the *DrawPolarPie* procedure is used in the example program ONEPIE.PAS.

In this example, *DrawPolarPie* first defines a window that is the size of the entire screen, with a header and border. Next, the array of values and optional text labels to be used in the creation of the pie chart are initialized. This part of the example is normally the only part that is application-specific. The size of each pie segment is specified by the *.area* entry in this array. This area is displayed as a percentage of the total area (determined by totalling all the other areas to be displayed in the pie). The numbers appropriate to your application are used here, and the *DrawPolarPie* procedure displays each segment according to its percentage of the whole pie. If you give any of the array entries a negative value, the pie drawing procedure will move this segment outward. This feature can be used to draw attention to important segments of the pie chart.

The *Mode* parameter allows you to display area values and/or text contained in *PieArray* as labels. These labels are usually displayed at the end of optional label lines. The area information is displayed exactly as passed in the array. If you don't want to display the numeric value of the segment, the *Mode* parameter allows you to display a text label only; the text is passed in the *PieArray*. The text label can include any alphanumeric character or ESCape sequence (used to specify special graphics characters). See the *DrawCartPie* and *DrawPolarPie* procedures in Chapter 3 for more information about this option.

The next part of the ONEPIE.PAS example determines the position, size, and shape of the pie to be drawn. The pie is specified by the coordinates of its center point, and radius and starting angle. (If the example were using the *DrawCartPie* procedure, the starting point would be specified by an [X,Y] position.)

The shape of the pie chart, like any other circle, is determined by its aspect ratio—its height-to-width ratio. You can vary the shape of the pie chart by calling the *SetAspect* procedure. In addition, a global constant, *AspectFactor*, sets the system-dependent aspect ratio, so that an aspect ratio of 1.0 produces a true circle on a particular hardware screen.

The parameters *InRadius* and *OutRadius* specify the inside and outside endpoints of the radial label line. This label line relates a text and numeric label with a particular pie segment. *InRadius* and *OutRadius* are referenced to the edge of the pie chart. A value of 1.0 puts the endpoint on the edge of the pie chart, a value of 0.5 puts the endpoint halfway between the edge and the center, and a value of 2.0 puts the endpoint at a distance of twice the radius out from the center of the chart. If both *InRadius* and *OutRadius* are 1.0, the label line is one dot long, coincides with the edge of the pie chart, and, thus, for all practical purposes, is not drawn.

The final parameters, *Mode* and *Size*, specify which labels, if any, are drawn, and their size. *Mode* allows four possibilities: no label, text label only, numeric label only, and both text and numeric label. *Size* specifies the scale of the label characters (multiples of 4x6 pixels).

```
program OnePieDemo;

{$I typedef.sys}              {these files must be}
{$I graphix.sys}             {included and in this order}
{$I kernel.sys}
{$I windows.sys}
{$I circsegm.hgh}
{$I pie.hgh}


procedure OnePieDem;

var sum,x1,y1,Radius,Theta,InRadius,OutRadius:real;
    n,Mode,Size:integer;
    a:PieArray;
    back:byte;
    ch:char;

begin
  ClearScreen;
  SetColorWhite;

  DefineWindow(1,0,0,XMaxGlb,YMaxGlb);
  DefineHeader(1,'A SINGLE PIE CHART');    {set up a window}
  DefineWorld(1,0,1000,1000,0);
  SelectWorld(1);
  SelectWindow(1);
  SetHeaderOn;
  SetBackground(0);
  DrawBorder;
```

```
n:=5;                                  {the number of pie segments}
a[1].area:=25;                         {initialize the pie array}
a[2].area:=17.5;
a[3].area:=9.6;
a[4].area:=21;
a[5].area:=35;
a[1].text:='JAN.=';
a[2].text:='FEB.=';
a[3].text:='MAR.=';
a[4].text:='APR.=';
a[5].text:='MAY=';

a[1].area:=-a[1].area;                 {move the first segment outward}

x1:=500;                               {set the center to mid screen}
y1:=500;

Radius:=200;                           {set the start of the circle}
Theta:=60;

SetAspect(1.0);                        {set the aspect ratio}

InRadius:=0.7;                         {set the ends of the label line}
OutRadius:=1.25;
Mode:=2;                               {set to draw both label}
Size:=2;                               {set to text size two}

DrawPolarPie(x1,y1,Radius,Theta,InRadius,OutRadius,a,n,Mode,Size);
                                       {draw the pie}

end;

begin
  InitGraphic;                         {initialize the graphics system}
  OnePieDem;                           {do the demo}
  repeat until KeyPressed;             {wait until a key is pressed}
  LeaveGraphic;                        {leave the graphics system}
end.
```

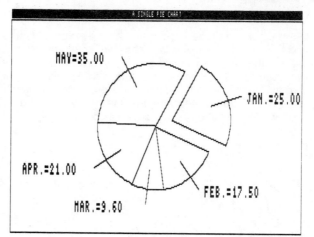

Figure 2-14: A Pie Chart (ONEPIE.PAS Example)

Bar Charts

Bar charts (histograms) are used to represent the way a given set of data changes over time. A bar chart displays a sequence of values as vertical bars, with each bar's height in proportion to the value associated with that bar. A bar chart is automatically generated by passing the array of the values to be displayed to the *DrawHistogram* procedure. The resulting bars are drawn adjacent to each other and always completely fill the width of the active window. The height of the bars is scaled by the world coordinate system active at the time.

The demo program ONEHIST.PAS is an example of the *DrawHistogram* procedure. This program draws ten random-length bars across a window that fills the screen. The procedure first fills the *PlotArray* with ten random values. The *PlotArray* is the same as that used to plot polygons, and therefore has two values in each array element (the *X* position and the *Y* displacement). The *X* value in this case is determined by the program, and the *Y* (vertical displacement) value is used by *DrawHistogram*.

Next, a window is defined and selected that fills the screen, and a world coordinate system is defined and selected that will determine the vertical scaling of the bar lengths. The *X* dimension specification can take any value except 0, since it is corrected for by the *DrawHistogram* routine.

The *Hatch* parameter specifies whether the bars are to be cross-hatched with slanting lines; *HatchDen* specifies the number of vertical pixels between each hatch line. The sign of *HatchDen* determines the direction of hatching; if it is negative, the first hatch line goes from lower left to upper right (positive slope); if it is positive, the first hatch line goes from upper right to lower left (negative slope); hatching direction alternates with each consecutive bar. In the call to *DrawHistogram*, a negative value for *DisplyLen* indicates that bars should be drawn from the *Y* zero axis (which is, in this case, at the bottom of the window). A positive value would specify that bars are always drawn from the bottom of the window, with negative values plotted as positive values.

```
program OneHist;

{$I typedef.sys}               {these files must be}
{$I graphix.sys}               {included and in this order}
{$I kernel.sys}
{$I windows.sys}
{$I hatch.hgh}
{$I histogrm.hgh}

procedure HistoDem;

var i,DisplyLen,HatchDen:integer;
    a:PlotArray;
    r:real;
    ch:char;
    Hatch:boolean;

begin
    DisplyLen:=10;                     {draw ten bars}

    for i:=0 to DisplyLen do {init the display array with random #'s}
      begin;
        a[i+1,2]:=random;
      end;
    SetColorWhite;                     {set up the window for the bar chart}
    SetBackground(0);
    SetHeaderOn;
    DefineWindow(1,0,0,XMaxGlb,YMaxGlb);
    DefineHeader(1,'A RANDOM BAR CHART WITH HATCHING');
    DefineWorld(1,-10,1.0,10,0);
    SelectWorld(1);
    SelectWindow(1);
    DrawBorder;                        {draw the window}
    Hatch:=true;                       {enable hatching}
    HatchDen:=7;                       {draw hatch lines this far apart}
    DrawHistogram(a,-DisplyLen,Hatch,HatchDen);   {draw the bar chart}
  end;
```

```
begin
   InitGraphic;                    {initialize the graphics system}
   HistoDem;                       {do the demo}
   repeat until KeyPressed;        {wait until a key is pressed}
   LeaveGraphic;                   {leave the graphics system}
end.
```

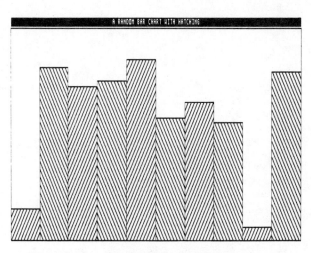

A RANDOM BAR CHART WITH HATCHING

Figure 2-15: A Bar Chart (ONEHIST.PAS Example)

The following example program (PIEHISTO.PAS on the distribution disk) shows both a bar and pie chart displaying the same data. An example of how to label bar charts is also included.

```
program PieHisto;

{$I typedef.sys}                   {these files must be}
{$I graphix.sys}                   {included and in this order}
{$I kernel.sys}
{$I windows.sys}
{$I circsegm.hgh}
{$I pie.hgh}
{$I hatch.hgh}
{$I histogrm.hgh}
```

```
procedure PieHistoDem;

var sum,x1,y1,x2,y2,InRadius,OutRadius:real;
    i,n:integer;
    a:PieArray;
    b:PlotArray;
    ch:char;
    NumText:WrkString;

begin

    n:=5;                               {the number of data points}
    a[1].area:=25;                      {initialize the pie array}
    a[2].area:=17.5;
    a[3].area:=9.6;
    a[4].area:=21;
    a[5].area:=35;
    a[1].text:='JAN. ';
    a[2].text:='FEB. ';
    a[3].text:='MAR. ';
    a[4].text:='APR. ';
    a[5].text:='MAY  ';

    for i:=1 to n do       {init the histogram array}
      b[i,2]:=a[i].area;

    ClearScreen;
    SetColorWhite;

    DefineWindow(1,0,0,XMaxGlb,YMaxGlb);
    DefineHeader(1,'BOTH A PIE AND A BAR CHART');   {set up a window}
    SelectWindow(1);
    SetHeaderOn;
    SetBackground(0);
    DrawBorder;

    for i:=1 to n do       {type the info in the  up-rt corner}
      begin
      GotoXY(60,4+i);                       {goto correct line}
      write(a[i].text,'=');                 {type the label info}
      str(a[i].area:6:2,NumText);           {format the numeric info}
      write(NumText);                       {type the numeric info}
      end;
```

```
DefineWindow(2,trunc(XMaxGlb/10),trunc(YMaxGlb/10),
            trunc(XMaxGlb*6/10),trunc(YMaxGlb*7/10));
DefineHeader(2,'A PIE CHART');           {set up a window}
DefineWorld(2,0,1000,1000,0);
SelectWorld(2);
SelectWindow(2);
SetHeaderOn;
SetBackground(0);
DrawBorder;

a[1].area:=-a[1].area;                   {move the first segment outward}
SetAspect(1.0);                          {set the aspect ratio}

x1:=500;                                 {set the center to mid screen}
y1:=500;

x2:=600;                                 {set the start of the circle}
y2:=350;

InRadius:=0.7;                           {set the ends of the label line}
OutRadius:=1.25;

DrawCartPie(x1,y1,x2,y2,InRadius,OutRadius,a,n,2,1); {draw the pie}

a[1].area:=-a[1].area;                   {reset the sign}

DefineWindow(3,trunc(XMaxGlb/2),trunc(YMaxGlb/2),
            trunc(XMaxGlb*9/10),trunc(YMaxGlb*9/10));
DefineHeader(3,'A BAR CHART');           {set up a window}
DefineWorld(3,0,60,10,0);
SelectWorld(3);
SelectWindow(3);
SetHeaderOn;
SetBackground(0);
DrawBorder;

DrawHistogram(b,n,true,5);

for i:=1 to n do          {draw the bar chart labels}
begin
DrawTextW((10/n)*(i-1),10,1,'   '+a[i].text);   {draw the text}
str(a[i].area:6:2,NumText);                      {format the number}
DrawTextW((10/n)*(i-1),16,1,' '+NumText);       {draw the number}
end;

end;
```

```
begin
   InitGraphic;                    {initialize the graphics system}
   PieHistoDem;                    {do the demo}
   repeat until KeyPressed;        {wait until a key is pressed}
   LeaveGraphic;                   {leave the graphics system}
end.
```

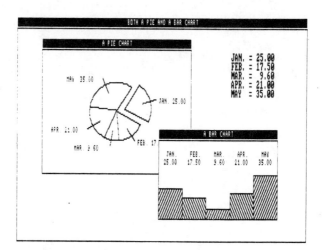

*Figure 2-16: Pie and Bar Chart Displaying Same Data
(PIEHISTO.PAS Example)*

Summary of Pie and Bar Chart Routines

DrawCircleSegment draws an arc of a circle with optional text and numeric labels

DrawCartPie draws a pie chart using Cartesian coordinates

DrawPolarPie draws a pie chart using polar coordinates

DrawHistogram draws a bar chart

Plotting Curves

Any curve that is made up of a series of points, usually connected by line segments, is called a *polygon*. By default (constant *MaxPlotGlb*), a polygon consists of a maximum of 100 points. If your application requires more points, the default for *MaxPlotGlb* can be changed, or, alternatively, multiple polygons can be used to create the final image. Because the resolution of a screen is limited, a smooth curve can usually be made out of a small number of line segments.

A Simple Example: Plotting a Sine Curve

The following example program (ONEPOLY.PAS on the distribution disk) plots a smooth sine curve using the *DrawPolygon* procedure. This example uses 30 line segments to produce the curve. In this case, the full screen is used; on the standard IBM graphics screen, there are approximately 20 pixels between the endpoints of the line segments. As can be seen from the graphics display output by this program, a smooth curve is drawn when this number of segments is used, with little evidence of where one line segment ends and another begins.

DrawPolygon receives its input as *X* and *Y* coordinates in the array *PlotArray*. This array is two dimensional—that is, each point's sequence in the curve is specified by the first dimension, and its *X* and *Y* values are selected by the second dimension. For example the value in the array *PlotArray*[5,1] would be the *X* position of the 5th point, and the value in *PlotArray*[5,2] would be the *Y* position.

A symbol can be optionally placed at each vertex point on the curve. If the value used to specify the symbol type is negative, the symbols are not connected by lines. The size of the symbols, and whether lines are drawn from the vertices to the *X* axis, are also specified by parameters passed to the procedure. See the *DrawPolygon* procedure description in Chapter 3 for detailed information about these options. This example simply draws a single sine curve across the screen. The array to draw is passed to *DrawPolygon* (with instructions to draw from the first to last point in the array) with no symbols at the vertices, and the curve is drawn as a series of line segments that connect the vertices.

The *PlotArray* for *DrawPolygon* is filled by the *GenerateFunction* procedure. Varying the value of *n* in this program varies the number of vertices in the curve. You can use the ONEPOLY.PAS example to experiment with the proper number of points needed to generate a smooth curve on your screen. In addition, you can draw a subset of the polygon by starting and ending the drawing on any element of this array; the indices of the desired start and end points are passed to the routine as parameters.

```
program OnePolygon;

{$I typedef.sys}                    {these files must be}
{$I graphix.sys}                    {included in this order}
{$I kernel.sys}
{$I windows.sys}
{$I polygon.hgh}


procedure PolygonDem;

var n:integer;
    b,a:PlotArray;
    ch:char;
    x1,x2:integer;

procedure GenerateFunction(var a,b:PlotArray;n:integer);

var i:integer;                      {generate a sine polygon}
    delta:real;

begin
  delta:=2*pi/(n-1);
  for i:=1 to n do
    begin
      a[i,1]:=(i-1)*delta-pi;
      a[i,2]:=sin(a[i,1]);
    end;
end;
```

```
begin
  ClearScreen;
  n:=30;
  GenerateFunction(a,b,n);                    {generate the polygon}

  DefineWindow(1,0,0,XMaxGlb,YMaxGlb);
  DefineHeader(1,'SINE CURVE AS A POLYGON');   {set up the screen}
  DefineWorld(1,-pi,1,pi,-1);
  SelectWorld(1);
  SelectWindow(1);
  SetBackground(0);
  SetHeaderOn;
  DrawBorder;
  DrawPolygon(a,1,n,0,0,0);                    {draw the polygon}
end;

begin
  InitGraphic;                                 {initialize the graphics system}
  PolygonDem;                                  {do the demo}
  repeat until KeyPressed;                      {wait until a key is pressed}
  LeaveGraphic;                                {leave the graphics system}
end.
```

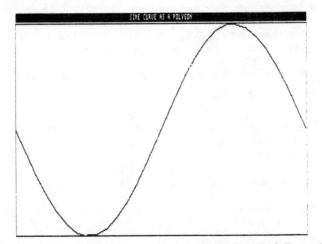

Figure 2-17: Plotting a Smooth Curve (ONEPOLY.PAS Example)

The DrawAxis Procedure

In many graphics applications that illustrate numeric results, it is useful to display a ruler that indicates the values of the displayed results. The *DrawAxis* procedure is used to draw rulers (and accompanying *X* and *Y* axes) along the left and bottom edges of the area that contains the graph. The rulers are scaled to fit the active window. *DrawAxis* automatically creates a new subwindow, bounded by the rulers, where drawing will take place. The world coordinate system (defined by the *DefineWorld* procedure) now fits in this subwindow.

Optional parameters passed to *DrawAxis* can provide a space between the rulers and the active window boundaries. This feature can also be used to provide space between legends or axis labels and the rulers, and/or to display multiple axes in one window. Other options can draw a border around the subwindow, turn the display of numeric labels and ruler tick marks on and off, draw zero *X* and *Y* axes, and select a line style for the axes.

The rulers have a couple of characteristics you should understand if you are to use them effectively. First, and most important, ruler markings are spaced according to screen pixel spacing. This means that the numbers associated with the rulers are correct with respect to the curve, but do not necessarily mark the decimal (or other number system) locations relevant to your application. In other words, ruler labels do not necessarily increment by one, ten, or other standard unit. In addition, with a higher resolution screen, (such as with the Hercules card), there will be more markings than with the same rulers drawn using a standard IBM graphics card.

The following example (ONEAXIS.PAS on the distribution disk) shows the simplest use of the *DrawAxis* procedure. This example defines a window that fills the whole screen, defines a world, and draws coordinate axes for the whole screen.

```
program OneAxis;

{$I typedef.sys}          {these files must be}
{$I graphix.sys}          {included and in this order}
{$I kernel.sys}
{$I windows.sys}
{$I axis.hgh}
```

```
procedure OneAxisDem;

begin
  ClearScreen;                        {init screen}
  SetColorWhite;
  SetBackground(0);

  DefineHeader(1,'LABELED AXES');     {define the window}
  SetHeaderOn;
  DefineWorld(1,-10,10,10,-10);
  SelectWorld(1);
  SelectWindow(1);
  DrawBorder;                         {draw it}
  DrawAxis(8,-7,0,0,0,0,0,0,true);    {draw coordinate axis}
end;

begin
  InitGraphic;                        {initialize the graphics system}
  OneAxisDem;                         {do the demo}
  repeat until KeyPressed;            {wait until a key is pressed}
  LeaveGraphic;                       {leave the graphics system}
end.
```

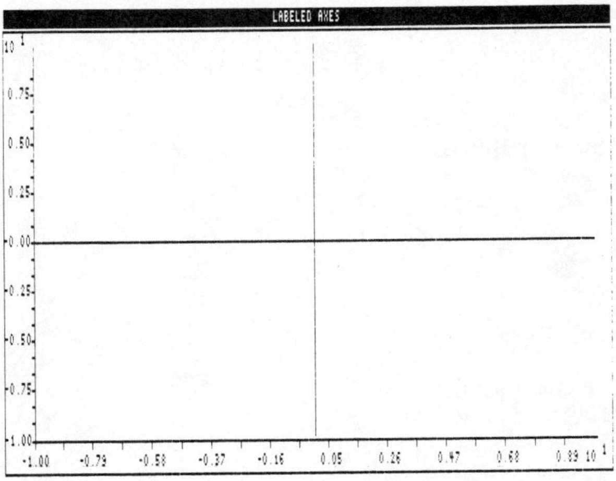

Figure 2-18: Labeled Axes (ONEAXIS.PAS Example)

Drawing a Sine Curve with Axes

The following example (POLYAXIS.PAS on the distribution disk) combines the previous two examples to display a sine curve inside axes that are bounded by the screen edges.

```
program OnePolygon;

{$I typedef.sys}                    {these files must be}
{$I graphix.sys}                    {included in this order}
{$I kernel.sys}
{$I windows.sys}
{$I axis.hgh}
{$I polygon.hgh}

procedure PolygonDem;

var n:integer;
    b,a:PlotArray;
    ch:char;
    x1,x2:integer;

procedure GenerateFunction(var a,b:PlotArray;n:integer);

var i:integer;                      {generate a sine polygon}
    delta:real;

begin
  delta:=2*pi/(n-1);
  for i:=1 to n do
    begin
      a[i,1]:=(i-1)*delta-pi;
      a[i,2]:=sin(a[i,1]);
    end;
end;
```

```
begin
  ClearScreen;

  n:=30;

  GenerateFunction(a,b,n);                      {generate the polygon}

  DefineWindow(1,0,0,XMaxGlb,YMaxGlb);
  DefineHeader(1,'SINE CURVE AS A POLYGON');    {set up the screen}
  DefineWorld(1,-pi,1,pi,-1);
  SelectWorld(1);
  SelectWindow(1);
  SetBackground(0);
  SetHeaderOn;
  DrawBorder;
  DrawAxis(8,-8,0,0,0,0,0,0,false);             {draw the axes}
  DrawPolygon(a,1,n,0,0,0);                      {draw the polygon}
end;

begin
  InitGraphic;                                  {initialize the graphics system}
  PolygonDem;                                   {do the demo}
  repeat until KeyPressed;                       {wait until a key is pressed}
  LeaveGraphic;                                 {leave the graphics system}
end.
```

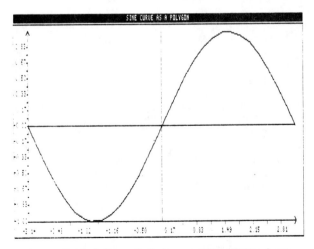
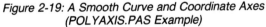

Figure 2-19: A Smooth Curve and Coordinate Axes
(POLYAXIS.PAS Example)

Polygon Modification Routines

There are several procedures that adjust the values in the *PlotArray* to *translate* (move), or rotate a polygon. These routines could be used for animation applications, to allow a single polygon to be used as the model for all the polygons that are to be subsequently moved about on the screen.

The example program (MOVEPOLY.PAS on the distribution disk) uses the *RotatePolygon* and *TranslatePolygon* procedures to draw an arrowhead on the screen, enable the cursor keys to rotate it, and move it forward and backward in the direction pointed to by the arrow. To end program execution, press the space bar.

The program initializes the polygon as an arrowhead in the center of the world, pointing towards the top of the screen. *RotatePolygon* rotates the polygon around its present "center of mass". This means that the polygon rotates around itself, rather than the origin (point [0,0]) of the coordinate system. To rotate the polygon about the origin (or any other point), use the *RotatePolygonAbout* procedure.

The *TranslatePolygon* procedure is used to move the arrowhead in the direction it is pointing. When the polygon is rotated, new increment values are used to translate the polygon in the new direction.

To move a polygon, you must first erase the old image before redrawing the new one. To do this, set the drawing color to black with the *SetColorBlack* procedure before calling *DrawPolygon* with the information from the last polygon.

There are no limits on where the polygon can be moved. Since the polygon is positioned using real coordinates, it would take a long time for this program to move the object to the end of the real number system. However, it does not take long to move the arrowhead off the screen. To make the program display the polygon in the world correctly, and to prevent the arrow from moving off the screen and destroying part of program memory, this program activates clipping by assigning a negative value to the last point to be displayed when calling *DrawPolygon*. When the arrowhead goes off the screen, *DrawPolygon* only draws the part of the line that fits the defined world.

```
program MovePolygon;
{$I typedef.sys}                        {these files must be}
{$I graphix.sys}                        {included in this order}
{$I kernel.sys}
{$I windows.sys}
{$I polygon.hgh}
{$I modpoly.hgh}

var ArrowAngle: integer;
    Ch: char;
    Arrow: PlotArray;
    CurrX,CurrY,IncrX,IncrY,Size,Speed: real;
    ArrowIncr: array[0..7,1..2] of real;

procedure MakeArrow;
begin
  Arrow[1,1]:=0;                        {PlotArray init for the arrowhead}
  Arrow[1,2]:=0;
  Arrow[2,1]:=Size;
  Arrow[2,2]:=-Size;
  Arrow[3,1]:=0;
  Arrow[3,2]:=Size;
  Arrow[4,1]:=-Size;
  Arrow[4,2]:=-Size;
  Arrow[5,1]:=0;
  Arrow[5,2]:=0;
end;

procedure MakeMoveTable;
begin
  ArrowIncr[0,1]:=0;                    {component velocities for radial moves}
  ArrowIncr[0,2]:=1;
  ArrowIncr[1,1]:=-1;
  ArrowIncr[1,2]:=1;
  ArrowIncr[2,1]:=-1;
  ArrowIncr[2,2]:=0;
  ArrowIncr[3,1]:=-1;
  ArrowIncr[3,2]:=-1;
  ArrowIncr[4,1]:=0;
  ArrowIncr[4,2]:=-1;
  ArrowIncr[5,1]:=1;
  ArrowIncr[5,2]:=-1;
  ArrowIncr[6,1]:=1;
  ArrowIncr[6,2]:=0;
  ArrowIncr[7,1]:=1;
  ArrowIncr[7,2]:=1;
end;
```

```
procedure MoveForward;                    {routine to move polygon forward}
begin
  SetColorBlack;                          {draw over old polygon to erase it}
  DrawPolygon(Arrow,1,-5,0,0,0);
  CurrX:=CurrX+IncrX;                     {move to new position}
  CurrY:=CurrY+IncrY;
  TranslatePolygon(Arrow,5,IncrX,IncrY);
  SetColorWhite;                          {draw polygon in new position}
  DrawPolygon(Arrow,1,-5,0,0,0);
end;

procedure MoveBack;                       {routine to move polygon back}
begin
  SetColorBlack;                          {same as above}
  DrawPolygon(Arrow,1,-5,0,0,0);
  CurrX:=CurrX-IncrX;
  CurrY:=CurrY-IncrY;
  TranslatePolygon(Arrow,5,-IncrX,-IncrY);
  SetColorWhite;
  DrawPolygon(Arrow,1,-5,0,0,0);
end;

procedure TurnLeft;                       {rotate polygon counter-clockwise}
begin
  SetColorBlack;                          {undraw old polygon}
  DrawPolygon(Arrow,1,-5,0,0,0);
  RotatePolygon(Arrow,5,45);              {rotate it 45 degrees}
  ArrowAngle:=ArrowAngle+1;
  if ArrowAngle>7 then ArrowAngle:=0;
  IncrX:=Speed * ArrowIncr[ArrowAngle,1];  {get new velocity}
  Incry:=Speed * ArrowIncr[ArrowAngle,2];
  SetColorWhite;                          {draw rotated polygon}
  DrawPolygon(Arrow,1,-5,0,0,0);
end;

procedure TurnRight;                      {rotate polygon clockwise}
begin
  SetColorBlack;                          {same as above}
  DrawPolygon(Arrow,1,-5,0,0,0);
  RotatePolygon(Arrow,5,-45);
  ArrowAngle:=ArrowAngle-1;
  if ArrowAngle<0 then ArrowAngle:=7;
  IncrX:=Speed * ArrowIncr[ArrowAngle,1];
  Incry:=Speed * ArrowIncr[ArrowAngle,2];
  SetColorWhite;
  DrawPolygon(Arrow,1,-5,0,0,0);
end;
```

```
begin
    InitGraphic;                              {initialize the graphics system}
    DefineWindow(1,0,0,XMaxGlb,YMaxGlb);
    DefineWorld(1,-1000,1000,1000,-1000);     {give it a world coord. system}
    SelectWorld(1);                           {select its world}
    SelectWindow(1);                          {select window}
    SetBackground(0);                         {give it a black background}
    Size:=100;
    Speed:=-30;
    CurrX:=0;
    CurrY:=0;
    ArrowAngle:=0;
    IncrX:=0;
    IncrY:=Speed;

    MakeArrow;                                {make the arrowhead}
    MakeMoveTable;                            {make the move table}
    DrawPolygon(Arrow,1,5,0,0,0);             {draw it pointing up}

repeat
    read(Kbd,Ch);                             {read the keystroke}
    case ord(Ch) of
        72 : MoveForward;                     {up arrow?}
        75 : TurnLeft;                        {left arrow?}
        77 : TurnRight;                       {right arrow?}
        80 : MoveBack;                        {down arrow?}
    end;
until Ch=' ';                                 {'space' char exits program}
LeaveGraphic;                                 {leave the graphics system}
end.
```

Finding a World to Fit a Polygon

In many applications that involve curves, the final form of the graph that is to be displayed is not known until the program is run. In these cases, the *FindWorld* procedure can be used to find the world coordinate system that will exactly fit the curve, or that is a specified percentage larger than the curve. *FindWorld* ensures that the area in which your curve is displayed is of the proper dimensions for your application. This procedure, in conjunction with the *DrawAxis* and *DrawPolygon* procedures, can produce a tailormade graphic presentation.

The *FindWorld* procedure always sets up a world with its lowest coordinates at the upper left corner of the window. The following code can be used after a call to *FindWorld* to turn the world coordinate system upside down:

```
with World[I] do    {integer I is the world being changed}
 begin
  Temp:=Y1;         {Temp is a real variable}
  Y1:=Y2;
  Y2:=Temp;
 end;
```

This must be done *before* selecting the world! (You can also flip the coordinate system horizontally by swapping the *X* coordinates *X1* and *X2*.)

Note: World coordinates in earlier versions of the Graphix Toolbox defined the *Y* axis using the Cartesian coordinate system. If you have a program written for an earlier version, you must switch the two *Y* parameters in each instance of *DefineWorld*, so that, for example,

```
DefineWorld(WorldNumber,X1,Y1,X2,Y2);
```

becomes

```
DefineWorld(WorldNumber,X1,Y2,X2,Y1);
```

The following program (FINDWRLD.PAS on the distribution disk) demonstrates *FindWorld* and some of the more advanced features of the *DrawPolygon* and *DrawAxis* routines. This program draws five random points on the screen with star symbols at each of the vertices, and axis rulers to show the scale of the numbers.

```
program FindWorld;

{$I typedef.sys}        {these files must be}
{$I graphix.sys}        {included in this order}
{$I kernel.sys}
{$I windows.sys}
{$I findwrld.hgh}
{$I axis.hgh}
{$I polygon.hgh}
{$I spline.hgh}
```

```
procedure FindWorldDem;

var x:real;
    dx,dy,i,n,lines,scale:integer;
    X1,Y1,X2,Y2:integer;
    b,a:PlotArray;

begin

    DefineWindow(1,0,0,XMaxGlb,YMaxGlb);   {define windows as whole screen}
    DefineWindow(2,0,0,XMaxGlb,YMaxGlb);
    DefineWorld(1,0,1000,1000,0);          {give a world to the screen}

    DefineHeader(2,'A FOUND WORLD');        {window where curve will go}
    SelectWindow(2);
    SetHeaderOn;

    n:=10;                                  {fill polygon array}
    for i:=1 to n do
      begin
        a[i,1]:=i-1;
        a[i,2]:=random-0.5;
      end;

    FindWorld(2,a,n,1,1.08);                {make world 2 the right size}

    SelectWindow(2);                        {select it and draw border}
    DrawBorder;

    dx:=-8;                                 {draw axis inset from window edge}
    dy:=7;
    X1:=3;
    Y1:=5;
    X2:=25;
    Y2:=10;
    lines:=0;
    scale:=0;

    SetLineStyle(0);                        {draw curve as solid line}
    DrawAxis(dx,dy,X1,Y1,X2,Y2,lines,scale,false);
    DrawPolygon(a,1,n,7,2,0);

    SelectWorld(1);                         {select outside window}
    SelectWindow(1);
```

```
DrawTextW(720,450,1,^['7@2   The data');          {print legend}
DrawTextW(720,550,1,'--  The curve');

end;

begin
  InitGraphic;                        {initialize the graphics system}
  FindWorldDem;                       {do the demo}
  repeat until KeyPressed;            {wait until a key is pressed}
  LeaveGraphic;                       {leave the graphics system}
end.
```

The special features of the *DrawAxis* procedure are used to make a
border around the drawing, and inset it from the edges of the active window. The inset feature can be used to make room for labels and
legends, and to allow multiple drawings in one window.

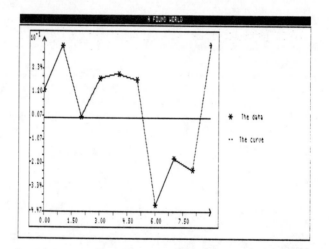

Figure 2-20: Finding a World for a Polygon (FINDWRLD.PAS Example)

Solving Curve-Fitting Problems

This section introduces you to the *Spline* and *Bezier* procedures. Both these procedures use polynomials to create curves. However, they are used for different reasons: the *Spline* procedure is used for fitting smooth curves to a given configuration of points, while *Bezier* is used to find the points that will create a desired curve. The *Spline* procedure is appropriate for many curve-fitting applications (for example, creating a smooth curve that intersects a set of experimental data), while *Bezier* is the procedure to use for line modeling and generating curves of arbitrary shape.

Fitting a Curve with the Spline Procedure

The curve produced by the FINDWRLD.PAS example is quite jagged; this is because the data points are connected by straight lines. The *Spline* procedure allows you to take the same set of points and find a smooth curve to fit that configuration of points. The general method used to find the function that will produce such a curve is called *interpolation*; using interpolation, you can generate the "missing" points that will smooth the curve.

The simplest way to interpolate a given set of points with a curve is the following: given *n* points [*X1,Y1*],[*X2,Y2*],[*X3,Y3*]...[*Xn,Yn*], we can interpolate the points with the n'th degree polynomial:

$$p_n(x) = y_1 \frac{(x-x_2) \cdots (x-x_n)}{(x_1-x_2) \cdots (x_1-x_n)} + y_2 \frac{(x-x_1)(x-x_3) \cdots (x-x_n)}{(x_2-x_1)(x_2-x_3) \cdots (x_2-x_n)}$$

$$+ \cdots + y_n \frac{(x-x_1) \cdots (x-x_{n-1})}{(x_n-x_1) \cdots (x_n-x_{n-1})}$$

This polynomial is known as the *Lagrange Interpolating Polynomial*, and it generates an exact curve that will pass through all the points. However, there is a problem inherent in this method of interpolation: it requires a formula with the same number of elements as the number of points to be intersected. Interpolating 90 points, for example, will yield a polynomial of degree 90, which is quite unwieldy.

A second, simpler approach to the problem is to fit a separate curve in each interval $[x_{i-1}, x_i]$, so that the curves meet with no jaggedness or irregularity. In other words, the function consists of pieces of polynomials that are patched together. The method used is known as *"Cubic Splines"*. Using this method, 3rd degree polynomials are used in each interval and patched together to form a "smooth" curve.

The Turbo Graphix *Spline* procedure uses this technique to interpolate the points that make up the curve. To produce the curve, the initial set of points is passed to the *Spline* procedure in the *PlotArray*, along with information about where to start and stop the interpolation, and a second *PlotArray* to receive the points of the smooth curve.

The following example (INTERP.PAS on the distribution disk) is essentially identical to the FINDWRLD.PAS example, except that an additional interpolated curve is plotted. Since the points are plotted at random, running the program several times will give you a good feel for how splines behave.

```
program Interpolate;

{$I typedef.sys}                     {these files must be}
{$I graphix.sys}                     {included in this order}
{$I kernel.sys}
{$I windows.sys}
{$I findwrld.hgh}
{$I axis.hgh}
{$I polygon.hgh}
{$I spline.hgh}


procedure SplineDem;

var x,temp:real;
    dx,dy,i,n,m,lines,scale:integer;
    X1,Y1,X2,Y2:integer;
    b,a:PlotArray;

begin

    DefineWindow(1,0,0,XMaxGlb,YMaxGlb)    {define both windows}
    DefineWindow(2,0,0,XMaxGlb,YMaxGlb);   {  as whole screen}
    DefineWorld(1,0,1000,1000,0);          {give a world to the screen}

    DefineHeader(2,'A  spline  interpolation'); {window where curves will go}
    SetHeaderOn;

    n:=12;                                 {fill polygon array}
    for i:=1 to n do
      begin
        a[i,1]:=i-1;
        a[i,2]:=random-0.5;
      end;
```

Compilibs, 2874 king


```
m:=50;                                  {generate spline with 50 points}
spline(a,n,a[2,1],a[n-1,1],b,m);
FindWorld(2,b,m,1,1.08);                {make world 2 the right size}
with World[2] do                        {flip the found world vertically}
  begin
    temp:=Y1;
    Y1:=Y2;
    Y2:=temp;
  end;
SelectWindow(2);                        {select it and draw border}
DrawBorder;

dx:=-8;                                 {draw axis inset from window edge}
dy:=7;
X1:=3;
Y1:=5;
X2:=25;
Y2:=10;
lines:=0;
scale:=0;

SetLineStyle(1);                        {draw  initial curve as dotted line}
DrawAxis(dx,dy,X1,Y1,X2,Y2,lines,scale,false);
DrawPolygon(a,2,n-1,7,2,0);             {don't draw the endpoints}

SetLineStyle(0);                        {draw interpolated curve as solid lin
DrawAxis(0,0,X1,Y1,X2,Y2,0,0,false);
DrawPolygon(b,1,-m,0,0,0);              {spline is not good on endpoints}

SelectWorld(1);                         {select outside window}
SelectWindow(1);

DrawTextW(730,400,1,^['7@2   The data');        {print legend}
DrawTextW(730,500,1,'..  The initial polygon');
DrawTextW(730,600,1,'__  The interpolated values');

end;

begin
  InitGraphic;                          {initialize the graphics system}
  SplineDem;                            {do the demo}
  repeat until KeyPressed;              {wait until a key is pressed}
  LeaveGraphic;                         {leave the graphics system}
end.
```

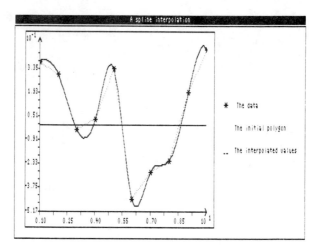

Figure 2-21: Finding a Smooth Curve with Cubic Splines
(INTERP.PAS Example)

Modeling a Curve with the Bezier Procedure

The *Bezier* procedure uses polynomials to solve the opposite problem that the *Spline* procedure handles: finding a set of points that will generate a predetermined curve. Bezier polynomials are defined by a given set of guiding (control) points. With the Bezier procedure, you continually redefine these control points so that they "pull on" the curve until it is of the desired shape. Once the guiding points are defined, if you have some talent for mathematics, you can easily find the equations for the corresponding Bezier polynomials that will draw the curve—that is, the algebraic formula for the curve drawn by this procedure. In addition, you can then use these points of the solution to plot the curves as polygons in other windows, using different coordinate systems, or on other screens on different computer systems.

The Bezier polynomial takes the following form:

$$p_x(t) = \sum_{i=0}^{m} C_i^m \, t^i \, (1-t)^{m-i} \, x_i$$

$$p_y(t) = \sum_{i=0}^{m} C_i^m \, t^i \, (1-t)^{m-i} \, y_i$$

where C_m^i is the number of combinations of *m* objects taken *i* at a time.

The following example (BEZIDEMO.PAS on the distribution disk) shows you how to use a set of control points to generate a desired curve. This technique is extremely useful for line modeling and some architectural applications. To illustrate the flexibility of the *Bezier* procedure, run this example program and try to make it loop twice.

```
program BeziDemo;

{$I typedef.sys}                        {these files must be}
{$I graphix.sys}                        {included and in this order}
{$I kernel.sys}
{$I windows.sys}
{$I axis.hgh}
{$I polygon.hgh}
{$I bezier.hgh}

procedure ClearToEol;                   {proc to clear to end of line}
var i: integer;

begin
  for i:=1 to 80 do write(' ');
end;

procedure BezierDem;

var result,i,MaxControlPoints,MaxIntPoints:integer;
    dummyx,dummyy:real;
    a,b:PlotArray;
    break:boolean;
    DummyS,Temp2,Temp:wrkstring;

begin

  MaxControlPoints:=7;                  {initialize everything}
  MaxIntPoints:=15;
  a[1,1]:=1;a[2,1]:=1.5;a[3,1]:=2;a[4,1]:=2.5;a[5,1]:=3;a[6,1]:=4;
  a[7,1]:=5;a[1,2]:=2;a[2,2]:=1.5;a[3,2]:=1;a[4,2]:=2.5;a[5,2]:=4;
  a[6,2]:=4.5;a[7,2]:=5;

  ClearScreen;                          {set up screen}
  SetColorWhite;
  DefineWorld(1,0,7.0,6.33,0);          {set world so rulers are good}
  SelectWorld(1);
  DefineWindow(1,0,0,XMaxGlb,17*YMaxGlb div 20);
```

```
SelectWindow(1);
SetBackground(0);
DrawBorder;
DrawAxis(7,-7,0,0,0,0,0,0,false);

break:=false;                            {init exit flag}

repeat
  SetLinestyle(1);                       {draw polygon between points}
  DrawAxis(0,0,0,0,0,0,0,0,false);       {do this so it lines up ok (no text)}
  DrawPolygon(a,1,MaxControlPoints,4,2,0);

  bezier(a,MaxControlPoints,b,MaxIntPoints);   {do bezier operation}

  SetLinestyle(0);                       {plot it}
  DrawAxis(0,0,0,0,0,0,0,0,false);
  DrawPolygon(b,1,MaxIntPoints,0,0,0);

  repeat
    gotoxy(1,24);                        {clear out old text}
    ClearToEol;
    gotoxy(1,25);
    ClearToEol;
    gotoxy(1,23);
    ClearToEol;
    gotoxy(1,23);                        {get point to change}
    write('Enter the number of the point to change :   ');
    gotoxy(43,23);
    read(Temp);
    val(Temp,i,result);
  until i in [0..MaxControlPoints];

  if i>0 then
    begin
      repeat
        gotoxy(1,24);                    {get new values for x and y}
        write('Old position : [',a[i,1]:4:2,',',a[i,2]:4:2,']');
        gotoxy(40,24);write('  New position  x:  ');
        gotoxy(60,24);
        read(DummyS);
        while DummyS[1]=' ' do delete(DummyS,1,1);
        Temp:=DummyS;
        gotoxy(40,25);write('  New position  y:  ');
        gotoxy(60,25);
```

```
        read(DummyS);
        while DummyS[1]=' ' do delete(DummyS,1,1);
        Temp2:=DummyS;val(Temp,dummyx,result);val(Temp2,dummyy,result);
        until ((dummyx>=X1WldGlb) and (dummyx<=X2WldGlb))
            and ((dummyy>=Y1WldGlb) and (dummyy<=Y2WldGlb));

        SetLinestyle(1);                    {undraw old curve}
        SetColorBlack;
        DrawAxis(0,0,0,0,0,0,0,0,false);
        DrawPolygon(a,1,MaxControlPoints,4,2,0);
        SetLinestyle(0);
        DrawAxis(0,0,0,0,0,0,0,0,false);
        DrawPolygon(b,1,MaxIntPoints,0,0,0);
        a[i,1]:=dummyx;a[i,2]:=dummyy;
        SetColorWhite;
      end
    else break:=true;                       {done?}
  until break;
end;

begin
  InitGraphic;                    {initialize the graphics system}
  BezierDem;                      {do the demo}
  LeaveGraphic;                   {leave the graphics system}
end.
```

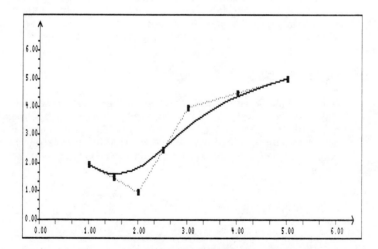

Figure 2-22: Finding Points to Fit a Smooth Curve of Predetermined Shape
(BEZIDEMO.PAS Example)

Summary of Polygon/Curve Routines

Bezier computes a smooth curve of predetermined shape from a set of control points

DrawAxis draws *X* and *Y* axes with ruler markings

DrawPolygon draws a polygon

FindWorld finds a world coordinate system to fit a given polygon

RotatePolygon rotates a polygon about its center of gravity

RotatePolygonAbout rotates a polygon about a given point

Spline computes a smooth curve from a set of control points

TranslatePolygon moves a polygon vertically and horizontally

Screens

There are two types of screens available for drawing with the Turbo Graphix Toolbox: the displayed screen, and a RAM (virtual) screen in memory. Turbo Graphix routines allow you to save and load either of these screens to and from disk, and restore them when you need them. You can also send images from either screen to your printer, and swap the contents of one screen with the contents of the other.

Saving and Loading Screens

Use the *SaveScreen* procedure to store the active screen as a file on disk. The single string parameter passed to the routine specifies the file name in which to save the screen contents. If a file with the same name already exists, it is overwritten. When you want to display the screen again, *LoadScreen* retrieves the screen from the file specified by its file name.

Both *SaveScreen* and *LoadScreen* use a format that is screen-type-specific; this means that a screen saved or loaded in a system with one graphics card may not keep its integrity if you attempt to retrieve or save it later on a system with another graphics card. This is also true with the *LoadWindowStack* and *StoreWindowStack* procedures; window stacks are not necessarily compatible between different versions of the Turbo Graphix Toolbox. However, there is no incompatibility between *individual windows*; you can safely store or load a window using the *LoadWindow* and *StoreWindow* procedures from one graphics screen type to another with no problems.

The following program example (SCREENIO.PAS on the distribution disk) demonstrates saving and loading a screen; included in this example is a routine that draws a Sierpinski curve. This screen image is stored to disk as file DEMO.PIC, the screen is cleared, and the image is read back to the screen. *SaveWindow/LoadWindow* and *SaveWindowStack/LoadWindowStack* can also be tested with this example. Simply substitute their names for the *SaveScreen* and *LoadScreen* procedures, and make sure the data you want to save and load is available.

```
program ScreenIO;

{$I typedef.sys}          {these files must be}
{$I graphix.sys}          {included in this order}
{$I kernel.sys}

procedure Sierpinski;

const n=5;
var i,h,x,y,x0,y0:integer;
    sec:boolean;

procedure plot;          {draw a line}

begin
  DrawLine(x,y,x0,y0);
  x0:=x;
  y0:=y;
end;
```

```
procedure b(i:integer); forward;    {forward references for recursion}

procedure c(i:integer); forward;

procedure d(i:integer); forward;

procedure a(i:integer);             {first recursive procedure}

begin
  if i>0 then
  begin
    a(i-1);
    x:=x+h;
    y:=y-h;
    plot;
    b(i-1);
    x:=x+2*h;
    plot;
    d(i-1);
    x:=x+h;
    y:=y+h;
    plot;
    a(i-1);
  end;
end;

procedure b;                        {second recursive procedure}

begin
  if i>0 then
  begin
    b(i-1);
    x:=x-h;
    y:=y-h;
    plot;
    c(i-1);
    y:=y-2*h;
    plot;
    a(i-1);
    x:=x+h;
    y:=y-h;
    plot;
    b(i-1);
  end;
end;
```

```
procedure c;                    {third recursive procedure}

begin
  if i>0 then
  begin
    c(i-1);
    x:=x-h;
    y:=y+h;
    plot;
    d(i-1);
    x:=x-2*h;
    plot;
    b(i-1);
    x:=x-h;
    y:=y-h;
    plot;
    c(i-1);
  end;
end;

procedure d;                    {last recursive procedure}

begin
  if i>0 then
  begin
    d(i-1);
    x:=x+h;
    y:=y+h;
    plot;
    a(i-1);
    y:=y+2*h;
    plot;
    c(i-1);
    x:=x-h;
    y:=y+h;
    plot;
    d(i-1);
  end;
end;
```

```
procedure DoIt;                        {sierpinski main procedure}

begin
  i:=3;
  h:=16;
  x0:=30;
  y0:=240;
  repeat
    i:=i+1;
    x0:=x0-h;
    h:=h div 2;
    y0:=y0+h;
    x:=x0;
    y:=y0;
    a(i-1);
    x:=x+h;
    y:=y-h;
    plot;
    b(i-1);
    x:=x-h;
    y:=y-h;
    plot;
    c(i-1);
    x:=x-h;
    y:=y+h;
    plot;
    d(i-1);
    x:=x+h;
    y:=y+h;
    plot;
  until i=n;
end;

begin                                  {sierpinski}
  SetHeaderOn;
  DefineWorld(1,-3,258,258,-3);
  SelectWorld(1);
  SelectWindow(1);
  DrawBorder;
  DoIt;
end;
```

```
begin
    InitGraphic;                           {initialize the graphics system}
    DefineHeader(1,'DEMONSTRATE SCREEN SAVE AND READ TO/FROM DISK');
    SetHeaderOn;                           {give it a header}
    Sierpinski;                            {do the curve}
    SaveScreen('DEMO.PIC');                {save the screen to disk}
    ClearScreen;                           {clear the screen}
    Delay(1000);     {delay so hard or RAM disk users can see the action}
    LoadScreen('DEMO.PIC');                {retrieve it from disk}
    repeat until KeyPressed;               {wait until a key is pressed}
    LeaveGraphic;                          {leave the graphics system}
end.
```

Printing Screens

There are two ways to print screen images. You can either use the Turbo Graphix *HardCopy* procedure, or the existing screen printing facility of your computer.

The *HardCopy* procedure prints screen images on any printer compatible with the Epson MX, RX, or FX series. Depending on the printer used, several width formats are available. These range from 640 points across the page to 1920 points. Since the standard IBM color graphics screen is 640 pixels wide, one screen will exactly fit across the page if the printer is able to print in the lowest resolution mode.

Some printers do not support all the available modes. For instance, the standard IBM, Epson MX-80-compatible printer will only print in the 960-points-per-line mode (mode 1). If you select any other mode for this printer, it will never enter graphics mode and will attempt to print the graphics screen in text characters.

Because of the different resolutions that are possible with *HardCopy*, the horizontal-to-vertical proportions (aspect ratio) of some images may be different on the screen than when the images are printed. Experiment with your printer and the resolution modes available to it to find what works best for you.

There is another way to print screen images using an IBM-compatible printer. First, install the graphics print routine that comes with the computer. Usually, this is done by running the system program GRAPHICS.COM that is on the MS-DOS system disk. Then, when you want to print a screen image, simply press the PrtSc key; on some keyboards, you must also press the Shift key.

There are a couple of advantages to using this program for printing screens. One is that it works on all Epson-like printers, and another is that it prints the image down the page rather than across it. The screen image fills the whole sheet, and the aspect ratio of the image is very close to that of the screen. Since the image is so large, fine details of the drawing look sharp and clear.

The following example program (SCRNPRNT.PAS on the distribution disk) prints out the screen image used in the SCREENIO.PAS example.

```
program ScreenIO;

{$I typedef.sys}                    {these files must be}
{$I graphix.sys}                    {included in this order}
{$I kernel.sys}

procedure Sierpinski;

const n=6;
var i,h,x,y,x0,y0:integer;
    sec:boolean;

procedure plot;                     {draw a line}

begin
  DrawLine(x,y,x0,y0);
  x0:=x;
  y0:=y;
end;

procedure b(i:integer); forward;    {forward references for recursion}
procedure c(i:integer); forward;
procedure d(i:integer); forward;
procedure a(i:integer);             {first recursive procedure}

begin
if i>0 then
  begin
    a(i-1);
    x:=x+h;
    y:=y-h;
    plot;
    b(i-1);
    x:=x+2*h;
    plot;
    d(i-1);
```

```
      x:=x+h;
      y:=y+h;
      plot;
      a(i-1);
    end;
end;

procedure b;                          {second recursive procedure}

begin
  if i>0 then
begin
      b(i-1);
      x:=x-h;
      y:=y-h;
      plot;
      c(i-1);
      y:=y-2*h;
      plot;
      a(i-1);
      x:=x+h;
      y:=y-h;
      plot;
      b(i-1);
    end;
end;

procedure c;                          {third recursive procedure}

begin
  if i>0 then
   begin
      c(i-1);
      x:=x-h;
      y:=y+h;
      plot;
      d(i-1);
      x:=x-2*h;
      plot;
      b(i-1);
      x:=x-h;
      y:=y-h;
      plot;
      c(i-1);
   end;
end;
```

```
procedure d;                    {last recursive procedure}

begin
  if i>0 then
  begin
    d(i-1);
    x:=x+h;
    y:=y+h;
    plot;
    a(i-1);
    y:=y+2*h;
    plot;
    c(i-1);
    x:=x-h;
    y:=y+h;
    plot;
    d(i-1);
  end;
end;

procedure DoIt;                 {sierpinski main procedure}

begin
  i:=3;
  h:=16;
  x0:=30;
  y0:=240;
  repeat
    i:=i+1;
    x0:=x0-h;
    h:=h div 2;
    y0:=y0+h;
    x:=x0;
    y:=y0;
    a(i-1);
    x:=x+h;
    y:=y-h;
    plot;
    b(i-1);
    x:=x-h;
    y:=y-h;
    plot;
```

```
      c(i-1);
      x:=x-h;
      y:=y+h;
      plot;
      d(i-1);
      x:=x+h;
      y:=y+h;
      plot;
    until i=n;
  end;

  begin   {sierpinski}
    SetHeaderOn;
    DefineWorld(1,-3,258,258,-3);
    SelectWorld(1);
    SelectWindow(1);
    DrawBorder;
    DoIt;
  end;

  begin
    InitGraphic;                            {initialize the graphics system}
    DefineHeader(1,'DEMONSTRATE SCREEN PRINTING'); {give it a header}
    SetHeaderOn;
    Sierpinski;                             {do the curve}
    HardCopy(false,1);                      {print it}
    repeat until KeyPressed;                {wait until a key is pressed}
    LeaveGraphic;                           {leave the graphics system}
  end.
```

Notes:

Chapter 3
TECHNICAL REFERENCE

This chapter provides detailed information about all the routines contained in the Turbo Graphix Toolbox. The first section gives an overview of the modular files that you'll need to include in your graphics application programs, along with a sample program. The following section defines and describes the constants and types used in the Turbo Graphix procedures, the third section provides a quick reference guide to Turbo Graphix routines, and the final section describes all the functions and procedures contained in the package.

Turbo Graphix Files

Turbo Graphix Toolbox is supplied on the distribution disk as an assortment of Turbo Pascal source files that you will need to "include" in your application program. These files are organized as modules to allow you to choose only the files you need for compilation into your final program.

If your system is equipped with a Hercules or IBM graphics card, the Turbo Graphix distribution disk will contain some files that are specific to your graphics card or computer system. Such files are named by a filename with an extension (.HRC for Hercules, .IBM for IBM) that indicates the graphics card the file is designed for. For instance, there is a GRAPHIX.IBM file that contains procedures for drawing, loading, and storing IBM screens, and a GRAPHIX.HRC file that contains the same procedures for Hercules screens. You must copy the GRAPHIX file written for your hardware (supplied on the distribution disk) onto the GRAPHIX.SYS file. This is done by invoking the Turbo Graphix batch program, i.e., type *tginst hgc* or *tginst ibm*. Failure to do so may cause malfunctioning of Turbo Graphix programs.

Basic System Files

The following files must be included in all Turbo Graphix applications, since they contain the global variable declarations, drawing primitives, and system routines that are necessary for drawing. The files must be included in the order given below.

TYPEDEF.SYS   Variable declarations for the Turbo Graphix Toolbox

GRAPHIX.SYS   Variables and routines for basic drawing, and for loading and storing screens

KERNEL.SYS   Primitives for control and initialization of the Turbo Graphix Toolbox

Supplemental System Files

These files are necessary for applications that use windows, text, or error messages. The only file that you have to include yourself is the WINDOWS.SYS file; the other files listed here will be used by your application automatically if they are needed.

WINDOWS.SYS   Routines for moving, loading and storing windows

8X8.FON   High-resolution font for IBM

14X9.FON   High-resolution font for Hercules

8x9.FON   High-resolution font for Zenith

4X6.FON   Turbo Graphix font

ERROR.MSG   Error message text

High-Level Command Files

The high-level routines are necessary for more complex graphics applications; you need only include the files you need for your particular application. All of the high-level files utilize the procedures contained in the basic system files; you must therefore include those files in order to utilize the high-level procedures.

Some of these high-level procedures rely on or work in conjunction with each other; in such cases, all the associated routines must be included in your application in the correct order. For instance, HISTOGRAM.HGH uses AXIS.HGH and PIE.HGH uses CIRCSEGM.HGH. To use either HISTOGRAM.HGH or PIE.HGH, you must first include the other high-level files that they use. Refer to specific routines listed in the final section of this chapter for other examples.

The high-level command files are as follows:

FINDWRLD.HGH   Procedure that finds a world coordinate system to fit a polygon

AXIS.HGH   Procedure that draws coordinate axes and labels

POLYGON.HGH   Procedure that draws polygons

MODPOLY.HGH   Procedures that rotate, scale and translate polygons

SPLINE.HGH   Procedure that does spline smoothing on polygons

BEZIER.HGH   Procedure that does Bezier interpolations on polygons

HATCH.HGH   Procedure that fills (hatches) bars in bar charts

HISTOGRM.HGH   Procedure that draws bar charts

CIRCSEGM.HGH   Procedure that draws and labels circle segments

PIE.HGH   Procedure that draws and labels pie charts

A Sample Turbo Graphix Toolbox Program

This sample program demonstrates the essential elements of a Turbo Graphix Toolbox program.

```
program simple;

{$I typedef.sys}              {these files must be}
{$I graphix.sys}              {included in this order}
{$I kernel.sys}

begin

    InitGraphic;              {initialize the graphics system}
    DrawBorder;               {draw a border around the drawing}
                              {area of the active window}
                              {(the dimensions of the active window}
                              {default to 640x200 points)}

    DrawLine(10,10,600,180);          {draw a line}
    DrawSquare(10,10,600,180,false);  {draw a square}
    DrawLine(-100,-20,750,320);       {draw a line to demonstrate}
                                      {clipping}

    repeat until KeyPressed;  {hold screen until key pressed}
    LeaveGraphic;             {leave the graphics system}
end.
```

Constant and Type Definitions

This section defines and describes, in alphabetical order, the constants and types used in Turbo Graphix Toolbox routines. Each constant or type is first defined, then described in detail as it applies to various procedures and functions. The Turbo Graphix file—either TYPEDEF.SYS or GRAPHIX.SYS—that contains the constant or type is given in brackets next to the constant or type name.

To customize your application, you can change some of the constants and types by altering the TYPEDEF.SYS or GRAPHIX.SYS file; however, this should be done with great care, and only after you have made certain that you thoroughly understand the Turbo Graphix Toolbox program. Otherwise, a system crash or other unpredictable disasters could occur.

AspectFactor [GRAPHIX.SYS]

Declaration   const AspectFactor:real = (depends on system);

Purpose   *AspectFactor* is used to adjust the aspect ratio (horizontal-to-vertical ratio) of a circle or ellipse so that a true circle is drawn on a particular physical screen using a particular graphics board. Without this adjustment, a circle may be drawn in a distorted way—too tall or too wide. This is because the horizontal-to-vertical ratio varies on different monitors.

Remarks   The graphics system multiplies the aspect ratio for a given circle or ellipse by the value of *AspectFactor* (which varies with the particular hardware screen installed) to create the desired shape. Multiplying *AspectFactor* by a constant creates ellipses with the same width, but with different heights. *AspectFactor* ✕ 1 creates a true circle on any screen, while *AspectFactor* ✕ 2 gives an ellipse that is twice as tall as it was, and *AspectFactor* ÷ 2 gives one that is half as tall as it was. Varying the aspect ratio varies the height of the drawn figure while keeping the width constant. Thus, if three circles are drawn with aspect ratios of *AspectFactor* ÷ 2, *AspectFactor*, and *AspectFactor* ✕ 2, respectively, the three figures will be tangent to each other at their leftmost and rightmost points, but not at their top and bottom points.

Remarks   This constant should not be altered, since it is specific to the graphics hardware in your system.

BackgroundArray [TYPEDEF.SYS]

Declaration   **type** BackgroundArray = array [0..7] of byte;

Purpose   *BackgroundArray* is used by the *SetBackground8* procedure to pass the specified 8x8 bit pattern for filling a window background.

CharFile [TYPEDEF.SYS]

Declaration   **const** CharFile: FileName = '4x6.font';

Purpose   *CharFile* contains the 4x6-pixel font.

Remarks   You can change this constant by altering either the TYPEDEF.SYS file or the main program before you call the *InitGraphic* procedure.

ConOutPtr [Turbo Pascal]

For information, please refer to the *Turbo Pascal Reference Manual* ("User Written I/O Drivers").

HardwareGrafBase [GRAPHIX.SYS]

Declaration   **const** HardwareGrafBase:integer = (depends on system);

Purpose   *HardwareGrafBase* defines the hardware segment address of graphics memory for a particular machine or graphics board.

HeaderSizeGlb [TYPEDEF.SYS]

Declaration   **const** HeaderSizeGlb: = 10;

Purpose   *HeaderSizeGlb* defines the vertical dimension, in pixels, of window headers. Its value must be greater than or equal to 6.

Remarks   The total vertical drawing area available in a given window is reduced by the size of its header.

IVStepGlb [GRAPHIX.SYS]

Declaration   const IVStepGlb:integer = (depends on system);

Purpose   *IVStepGlb* specifies the initial value of *VStep*, the step size (increment) by which windows are moved vertically.

Remarks   *IVStep* is used by the Turbo Graphix program to speed the vertical movement of large windows. Its value varies according to the particular hardware installed. See the *MoveVer* and *SetVStep* procedures.

MaxBackground [GRAPHIX.SYS]

Declaration   const MaxBackground:integer = (depends on system);

Purpose   *MaxBackground* is a value that specifies the maximum number of available background ("black") colors for a particular hardware configuration: 0 or 15 for IBM versions, 0 for Hercules, and 0 for Zenith.

Remarks   This constant should not be changed, since it is specific to the graphics hardware installed.

MaxForeground [GRAPHIX.SYS]

Declaration   const MaxForeground:integer = (depends on system);

Purpose   *MaxForeground* is a value that specifies the maximum number of available foreground ("white") drawing colors for a particular hardware configuration: 15 for IBM (except the PCjr version, which allows only black or white), 0 for Hercules, and 7 for Zenith.

Remarks   This constant should not be changed, since it is specific to the graphics hardware installed.

It is illegal to set the foreground and background colors to the same value. See the *SetBackgroundColor* and *SetForegroundColor* procedures for more information.

MaxPiesGlb [TYPEDEF.SYS]

Declaration   const MaxPiesGlb = 10;

Purpose   *MaxPiesGlb* specifies the maximum number of sections allowed in a pie chart.

MaxPlotGlb [TYPEDEF.SYS]

Declaration   const MaxPlotGlb = 100;

Purpose   *MaxPlotGlb* defines the maximum number of points in a *PlotArray*.

Remarks   *PlotArray* is used to store the vertices of polygons. *Bezier, DrawHistogram, DrawPolygon, FindWorld, RotatePolygon, ScalePolygon, Spline,* and *TranslatePolygon* make use of the *MaxPlotGlb* constant.

MaxWindowsGlb [TYPEDEF.SYS]

Declaration   const MaxWindowsGlb = 16;

Purpose   *MaxWindowsGlb* specifies the maximum number of defined windows.

MaxWorldsGlb [TYPEDEF.SYS]

Declaration   const MaxWorldsGlb = 4;

Purpose   *MaxWorldsGlb* specifies the maximum number of world coordinate systems that can be defined.

Remarks   Only one world coordinate system can be used at one time.

MinBackground [GRAPHIX.SYS]

Declaration   **const** MinBackground:integer = (depends on system);

Purpose   *MinBackground* specifies the minimum value for the background ("black") color for a particular graphics card: 0 for IBM, 0 for Hercules, and 0 for Zenith.

Remarks   This constant should not be changed, since it is specific to the graphics hardware installed.

MinForeground [GRAPHIX.SYS]

Declaration   **const** MinForeground:integer = (depends on system);

Purpose   *MinForeground* specifies the minimum value for the foreground ("white") drawing color for a particular graphics card: 1 for IBM, 1 for Hercules, and 1 for Zenith.

Remarks   This constant should not be changed, since it is specific to the graphics hardware installed.

PieArray [TYPEDEF.SYS]

Declaration   **type** PieArray = array [1..MaxPiesGlb] of PieType;

Purpose   *PieArray* is used to pass the definition of a pie chart to the *DrawCartPie* and *DrawPolarPie* procedures; each element of the array defines a single section of the pie. The two fields in the array are *Area* (a real number), and *Text* (a string).

Remarks   The maximum number of pie sections is determined by the *MaxPiesGlb* constant.

PlotArray [TYPEDEF.SYS]

Declaration   **type** PlotArray = array [1..MaxPlotGlb, 1..2] of real;

Purpose   *PlotArray* specifies the vertices of a given polygon, and is used to pass polygons to a procedure.

Remarks   In the Turbo Graphix Toolbox, the term *polygon* can mean any ordered collection of points, possibly (but not necessarily) connected by lines. Thus, a sampling of a sine wave can be called a polygon, though a smooth sine wave with an infinite number of points cannot. The data structure simply contains points. Poly[*i*,1] is the *i*'th *X* coordinate, and Poly[*i*,2] is the *i*'th *Y* coordinate. The maximum number of points in a polygon is determined by the constant *MaxPlotGlb*.

     PlotArray is used by *Bezier*, *DrawHistogram*, *DrawPolygon*, *FindWorld*, *RotatePolygon*, *ScalePolygon*, *Spline*, and *TranslatePolygon*.

RamScreenGlb [TYPEDEF.SYS]

Declaration   **const** RamScreenGlb:boolean = true;

Purpose   *RamScreenGlb* determines whether or not a RAM (virtual) screen is allocated for drawing.

Remarks   A RAM screen takes up a large chunk of memory (as defined by the constant *ScreenSizeGlb*, in bytes) but it enables you to do many things, such as two-screen animation and smooth window movement over a background (see the *MoveWindow* procedure).

     Some hardware configurations allocate dedicated memory for RAM screens; in those cases, *RamScreenGlb* will always be TRUE. See Appendix A for further information.

ScreenSizeGlb [GRAPHIX.SYS]

Declaration   const ScreenSizeGlb:integer = (depends on system);

Purpose   *ScreenSizeGlb* specifies the size of the screen (in bytes divided by 2) for a particular hardware configuration.

Remarks   This constant should not be altered, since it is specific to the size of the physical screen in your computer; any change to this constant may cause a system crash or unnecessary memory allocation.

StringSizeGlb [TYPEDEF.SYS]

Declaration   const StringSizeGlb = 80;

Purpose   *StringSizeGlb* specifies the maximum string length of the type *WrkString*.

Remarks   This constant is used by any procedure that requires a text string.

WrkString [TYPEDEF.SYS]

Declaration   type WrkString = string[StringSizeGlb];

Purpose   *WrkString* is the string type used by Turbo Graphix procedures that either require string parameters, or use strings internally.

Remarks   The *DefineHeader* and *DrawText* procedures use *WrkString* as their principle parameter.

XMaxGlb [GRAPHIX.SYS]

Declaration | const XMaxGlb:integer = (depends on system);

Purpose | *XMaxGlb* specifies the width of the screen in bytes, less 1; that is, the maximum value of an *X* (horizontal) window definition coordinate. The maximum screen width is $XMaxGlb \times 8 + 7$.

Remarks | This constant should not be changed, since it is specific to the particular hardware configuration.

The *DefineWindow* procedure uses *XMaxGlb* to check whether a window is being defined within the physical screen.

XScreenMaxGlb [GRAPHIX.SYS]

Declaration | const XScreenMaxGlb:integer = (XMaxGlb*8+7)

Purpose | *XScreenMaxGlb* specifies the maximum width of the screen for a particular hardware configuration.

Remarks | This constant should not be changed, since it is specific to the particular hardware configuration.

YMaxGlb [TYPEDEF.SYS]

Declaration | const YMaxGlb:integer = (depends on system);

Purpose | *YMaxGlb* specifies the height of the screen in pixels; that is, the maximum value of a Y (vertical) absolute screen coordinate.

This constant should not be changed, since it is specific to the particular hardware configuration.

The *DefineWindow* procedure uses *YMaxGlb* to check whether a window is being defined within the physical screen.

Quick Reference Guide to Turbo Graphix Routines

In the following list, the Turbo Graphix Toolbox routines are grouped by function into six sections: Initialization and Error, Screens, Windows, Color and Drawing, Text, and Internal. Since the list is designed to help you find routines according to their logical use, and since some routines logically relate to more than one function, a few routines appear in more than one section. The declaration for each routine is listed, followed by its page number.

Initialization and Error

Screens

Windows

Color and Drawing

Text

Internal

Procedures and Functions

This section defines and describes, in alphabetical order, all the procedures and functions contained in the Turbo Graphix Toolbox. The call-up for each procedure or function is given, followed by a detailed description of its function. Remarks, restrictions, and examples are given where appropriate, as well as cross-referencing to related procedures and functions. The Turbo Graphix file that contains the procedure or function is given in brackets next to the name of the procedure or function.

Refer to page 94 for a description of the constants and types used in these procedures and functions.

If your system contains an IBM or Hercules graphics card, you must copy the GRAPHIX file written for your hardware (supplied on the distribution disk) onto the GRAPHIX.SYS file. This is done by invoking the Turbo Graphix batch program, i.e., type *tginst hgc* or *tginst ibm*. Failure to do so may cause malfunctioning of Turbo Graphix programs.

BaseAddress [GRAPHIX.SYS]

Declaration	**function** BaseAddress(Y:integer):integer;
Usage	BaseAddress(Y);
Parameters	*Y* : a screen line (0...YMaxGlb)
Function	*BaseAddress* calculates the offset of screen line *Y* in memory.
Remarks	This function is for internal use by the graphics system.
Restrictions	None
Example	I:=BaseAddress(5); *I* is the offset at the start of screen line 5 (the sixth line on the screen).

FillChar(Mem[GrafBase:BaseAddress(9)],XMaxGlb,0);
sets the 10th screen line to "black."

Bezier [BEZIER.HGH]

Declaration	**procedure** Bezier(A:PlotArray;N:integer; **var** B:PlotArray;M:integer);

Usage   Bezier(A,N,B,M);

Parameters   *A*: array of *X* and *Y* control points
N: number of control points
B: array of resultant Bezier-function base points
M: desired number of base points in resultant Bezier polynomial curve

Function   *Bezier* computes a Bezier polynomial curve from an array, *A*, that contains *N* control points. The resultant array, *B*, is filled with *M* base points that constitute a parametric curve. The curve passes through the first and last control points, and passes as close as possible to each of the other points.

A Bezier function is defined by a set of control points (*X* and *Y* values). Within this defined interval, the Bezier function calculates the resultant base points.

Remarks   Bezier polynomials are often used when a smooth curve of some particular form is needed. Increasing the value of *M* smooths the curve, but slows down the computing process.

The specific attributes of Bezier functions and their applications in graphic design are discussed in the book, *Principles of Computer Graphics*, by W. Newmann and R.Sproul.

Restrictions   The maximum values for *N* and *M* are determined by the constant *MaxPlotGlb*, specified in the TYPEDEF.SYS file. The default value is 100 (of *MaxPlotGlb*).

See Also   DrawPolygon
RotatePolygon
ScalePolygon
TranslatePolygon

Example

This example, taken from the Turbo Graphix demo program, uses seven control points to draw a curve. Fifteen base points (shown as a dotted line) are generated by this procedure. The positions of the points and the value of *M* can be changed interactively.

```
program BezierDemo;
{$itypedef.sys}
{$igraphix.sys}
{$ikernel.sys}
{$ibezier.hgh}
{$ipolygon.hgh}

const
    ControlPoints=7;

var
    A,B: PlotArray;
    NewX,NewY: real;
    I,BezierPoints: integer;

begin
InitGraphic;
SetHeaderOn;
    BezierPoints:=15;
    A[1,1]:=1;A[2,1]:=1.5;A[3,1]:=2;A[4,1]:=2.5;A[5,1]:=3;
A[6,1]:=4;A[7,1]:=5;
    A[1,2]:=2;A[2,2]:=1.5;A[3,2]:=1;A[4,2]:=2.5;A[5,2]:=4;
A[6,2]:=4.5;A[7,2]:=5;
DefineWorld(1,0,0,6,6);
    SelectWorld(1);
    DefineWindow(1,0,0,79,170);
    SelectWindow(1);
    DefineHeader(1,'BEZIER PROCEDURE DEMONSTRATION');
    repeat
        ClearScreen;
        DrawBorder;
        SetLinestyle(1);
        DrawPolygon(A,1,ControlPoints,4,2,0);
        Bezier(A,ControlPoints,B,BezierPoints);
        SetLinestyle(0);
        DrawPolygon(B,1,BezierPoints,0,0,0);
        gotoxy(1,23);
```

```
  write('Enter point # to change (0 to change # of Bezier points): ');
  readln(I);
  if I in [1..ControlPoints] then
   begin
    repeat
      gotoxy(1,24);
      write('Old position:[',A[I,1]:4:2,',',A[I,2]:4:2,']');
      gotoxy(40,24);write('New position x:');
      readln(NewX);
      gotoxy(40,25);write('New position y:');
      readln(NewY);
     until (NewX>=0) and (NewX<=6) and (NewY>=0) and (NewY<=6);
     A[I,1]:=NewX;
     A[I,2]:=NewY;
    end
   else if I=0 then
    begin
     gotoxy(1,24);
     write('Old density: ',BezierPoints,'  New density: ');
     readln(BezierPoints);
    end;
 until not (I in [0..ControlPoints]);
 LeaveGraphic;
end.
```

ClearScreen [KERNEL.SYS]

Declaration **procedure** ClearScreen;

Usage ClearScreen;

Function *ClearScreen* erases the screen that is currently in use (the active screen).

Remarks Initialization is not performed by this procedure; see *InitGraphic*.

Restrictions None

See Also InitGraphic

Example
```
program ClearScreenExample;
{$itypedef.sys}
{$igraphix.sys}
{$ikernel.sys}
begin
  DrawLine(1,1,200,200);
  DrawLine(1,200,200,1);
  gotoxy(50,12);
  write('Hit return to clear screen: ');
  readln;
  ClearScreen;
  gotoxy(10,25);
  write('Hit return to end: ');
  readln;
end.
```

ClearWindowStack [WINDOWS.SYS]

Declaration	**procedure** ClearWindowStack(Nr:integer);
Usage	ClearWindowStack(Nr);
Parameters	*Nr*: index of window to be erased [1..*MaxWindowsGlb*]
Function	*ClearWindowStack* deletes a designated window, *Nr*, from the window stack. If there is no window entry at the given index, the operation is not performed.
Remarks	A call to *RestoreWindow* cannot restore a window erased using this routine.
Restrictions	The value of *Nr* must lie between 1 and the constant *MaxWindowsGlb* (defined in the TYPEDEF.SYS file).
See Also	ResetWindowStack RestoreWindow StoreWindow
Example	ClearWindowStack(7); removes the window stack entry (if there is one) for window 7.

Clip [KERNEL.SYS]

Declaration	**function** Clip(var X1,Y1,X2,Y2:integer):boolean;

Usage   Clip(X1,Y1,X2,Y2);

Parameters

X1,Y1 : coordinates of starting point of line
X2,Y2 : coordinates of end point of line
boolean : if FALSE, line lies outside window

Function

Clip clips a line to fit the active window, and determines whether or not the full length of a line is drawn. The four integer variables represent absolute screen coordinates. Clip adjusts them as follows: if a line is drawn from [*X1,Y1*] to [*X2,Y2*], any part of the line that lies outside the active window is removed. The resulting coordinates describe a line that is entirely contained by the active window. The boolean function value is TRUE if the adjusted coordinates still represent a line, and FALSE if the entire line is clipped away.

Remarks

Although this function is mainly for internal use, it can also be useful when you are working with window mode off (*SetWindowModeOff*), to ensure that drawings remain within the physical screen.

Restrictions

Since the four integer parameters are modified by *Clip*, they must be variables; they cannot be expressions.

See Also

Clipping
SetClippingOff
SetClippingOn
SetWindowModeOff
SetWindowModeOn

Example

if Clip(X1,Y1,X2,Y2) **then** DrawLine(X1,Y1,X2,Y2);
    draws only the part of the line that falls within the active window.

B:=Clip(X1,Y1,X2,Y2);
    adjusts [X1,Y1] and [X2,Y2] so that the line between them is entirely contained by the active window; sets B to TRUE if any part of the original line remains.

Clipping [KERNEL.SYS]

Declaration	**function** Clipping:boolean;
Usage	Clipping;
Function	*Clipping* returns the clipping status: TRUE when clipping is enabled with the *SetClippingOn* procedure; FALSE when clipping is disabled with the *SetClippingOff* procedure.
Restrictions	None
See Also	Clip SetClippingOn SetClippingOff
Example	B:=Clipping; sets *B* to TRUE if clipping is enabled, FALSE if not.

CopyScreen [KERNEL.SYS]

Declaration	**procedure** CopyScreen;
Usage	CopyScreen;
Function	*CopyScreen* copies the active screen onto the inactive screen.
Remarks	If the active screen is the RAM screen, this procedure copies it to the displayed screen. *CopyScreen* is often used to save a window background when another window is being moved over the background. See Chapter 2, page 39 for detailed information about moving windows.
Restrictions	In order to use this procedure, there must be an available RAM screen in memory, i.e, the constant *RamScreenGlb* must be TRUE in the TYPEDEF.SYS file.
See Also	LoadScreen SaveScreen SelectScreen SetBackground SwapScreen
Example	CopyScreen; copies the active screen onto the inactive screen.

CopyWindow [WINDOWS.SYS]

Declaration   **procedure** CopyWindow(From,To:byte; X1,Y1:integer);

Usage   CopyWindow(From,To,X1,Y1);

Parameters

From : screen from which window is copied
To : screen window is to be copied onto
X1, Y1 : window definition coordinates where window is copied

Function

CopyWindow copies the contents of the active window to and from the RAM screen and the displayed screen. A value of 1 for *To* or *From* designates the displayed screen, while a value of 2 for *To* or *From* designates the RAM screen. The window is copied to the screen location specified by window definition coordinates [*X1,Y1*].

Remarks

CopyWindow copies images from the area enclosed by the active window in the specified screen. This may have surprising results if the wrong screen is specified!

See page 39 for complete information about moving windows.

Restrictions

To use *CopyWindow*, there must be an available RAM screen in memory, i.e. the constant *RamScreenGlb* is TRUE (defined in the TYPEDEF.SYS file).

See Also

LoadWindow
SelectWindow

Example

CopyWindow(1,2,10,20);
copies the active window from the displayed screen to the RAM screen, placing the upper left corner of the window at window definition coordinates [10,20] (screen coordinates [80,20]).

CopyWindow(1,1,50,5);
copies the active window from its current position on the displayed screen to window definition coordinates [50,5] (screen coordinates [400,5]) on the displayed screen.

DC [GRAPHIX.SYS]

Declaration	**procedure** DC(C:byte);
Usage	DC(C);
Parameter	*C*: ASCII code of drawn character
Function	*DC* draws the character whose ASCII code is *C* at text coordinates [*XTextGlb,YTextGlb*] (internal variables) in the font used by the particular hardware configuration installed.
Remarks	*DC* is for internal use by the graphics system. It does not advance the cursor.
Restrictions	None
See Also	DefineTextWindow TextDown TextLeft TextRight TextUp
Example	DC(32); displays character 32 (space) at the current cursor position on the active screen, without moving the cursor.

DefineHeader [KERNEL.SYS]

Declaration   **procedure** DefineHeader(I:integer; Hdr:WrkString);

Usage   DefineHeader (I,Hdr);

Parameters   *I*   : index of window for which header is defined
               [1..*MaxWindowsGlb*]
               Hdr : string term for window header

Function   *DefineHeader* defines a window header, *Hdr*, for a given
               window, *I*. The procedure defines the text that makes up
               the header, but has no effect on the display; the header
               is not displayed or altered until procedure *DrawBorder* is
               called. The header is then centered horizontally either on
               the top or the bottom of the window, depending on
               whether the last call was to *SetHeaderToTop* or
               SetHeaderToBottom.

Restrictions   Window headers can only be drawn with the 4x6-pixel
               character set.

               The value of *I* must lie between 1 and the constant
               MaxWindowsGlb (defined in TYPEDEF.SYS file).

See Also   DrawBorder
               RemoveHeader
               SetHeaderOff
               SetHeaderOn
               SetHeaderToBottom
               SetHeaderToTop

Example   DefineHeader(1,'*** Edit window ***');
               defines the header of window 1 to be *** *Edit window*
               ***, without affecting the display of the header.

DefineTextWindow [KERNEL.SYS]

Declaration   **procedure** DefineTextWindow(I,Left,Up,Right,Down,
                     Border:integer);

Usage   DefineTextWindow(I,Left,Up,Right,Down,Border);

Parameters   *I*   : index of window
                     Left   : *X* coordinate of left edge of machine-dependent
                               text
                     Up   : *Y* coordinate of upper edge of machine-
                               dependent text
                     Right : *X* coordinate of right edge of machine-
                               dependent text
                     Down   : *Y* coordinate of bottom edge of machine-
                               dependent text
                     Border : desired number of pixels between text and
                               window boundaries

Function   *DefineTextWindow* uses the given text coordinates (*Left,
                     Up, Right, Down, and Border*) and the number of pixels,
                     Border, that you want between the text and all four
                     edges of the window, to define a window. The window
                     defined will allow for a uniform space between the text
                     and the window edges.

Remarks   *DefineTextWindow* is used to fit and align text within a
                     window. It is particularly useful with the Hercules version
                     of the Turbo Graphix Toolbox, since Hercules text is
                     defined on 9-pixel boundaries, while windows are defined
                     on 8-pixel boundaries; this one-pixel offset can create
                     alignment problems.

                     If you wish to vary the space between your text and any
                     of the four window edges, use the *TextLeft, TextRight,
                     TextUp,* and *TextDown* functions to define the space in-
                     dividually for each window edge.

Restrictions   If you define a 4x6-pixel header for your window, the place-
                     ment of the machine-dependent text will be thrown off by
                     the size of the header; in this case, use the four functions
                     mentioned above to realign text within the window.

                     Note that the horizontal border values are only approxi-
                     mate, since they are restricted to window defintion coor-
                     dinates, and are adjusted outward if necessary.

See Also   DefineHeader
                DefineWindow
                TextDown
                TextLeft
                TextRight
                TextUp

Example   DefineTextWindow(3,2,2,79,24,4);
                defines window 3 so that it encloses text coordinates
                from [2,2] to [79,24], with a border of at least 4 pixels
                between the text and all edges.

DefineWindow [KERNEL.SYS]

Declaration   **procedure** DefineWindow(I,XLow,YLow,XHi,YHi:integer);

Usage   DefineWindow(I,XLow,XHi,YHi);

Parameters   *I*   : index of window [1..*MaxWindowsGlb*]
XLow : *X* value of upper left window position
        [0..*XMaxGlb*]
YLow : *Y* value of upper left window position
        [0..*YMaxGlb*]
XHi   : *X* value of lower right window position
        [1..*XMaxGlb*]
YHi   : *Y* value of lower right window position
        [0..*YMaxGlb*]

Function   *DefineWindow* defines a region of the screen as a window, *I*. The window is defined as a rectangle with the upper left corner at [*XLow,YLow*] and the lower right corner at [*XHi,YHi*].

Remarks   The *X* coordinates of a window are defined in 8-pixel chunks; i.e, windows are placed on byte boundaries in memory. If *DefineWindow* is called with parameters (1,10,10,19,19), the defined window is 10 pixels tall and 80 pixels wide.

Restrictions   The value of *I* must be between 1 and *MaxWindowsGlb* (as defined in the TYPEDEF.SYS file), all coordinates must lie within the physical screen, and the *Low* coordinates must be lower in numeric value than the *Hi* coordinates; otherwise, an error will occur.

See Also   RedefineWindow
SelectWindow

Example   DefineWindow(4,5,5,10,10);
defines window 4 , with upper left corner at window definition coordinates [5,5] and lower right corner at [10,10] (screen coordinates [40,5] and [87,10]).

DefineWindow(2,0,0,XMaxGlb div 2,YMaxGlb div 2);
defines window 2 as the upper left quarter of the screen.

DefineWorld [KERNEL.SYS]

Declaration	**procedure** DefineWorld(I:integer; XLow,YLow,XHi,YHi:real);

Usage   DefineWorld(I,XLow,YLow,XHi,YHi);

Parameters
    I   : index of world to be defined [1...*MaxWorldsGlb*]
    XLow : *X* coordinate of upper left vertex
    YLow : *Y* coordinate of upper left vertex
    XHi   : *X* coordinate of lower right vertex
    YHi   : *Y* coordinate of lower right vertex

Function   *DefineWorld* defines a world coordinate system, delineated by the rectangle formed by the vertices [*XLow,YLow*] and [*XHi,YHi*]. World coordinates therefore range from [*XLow,YLow*] to [*XHi,YHi*].

Remarks   The world coordinate system is not enabled until *SelectWorld* is called.

Restrictions   The world's index value, *I*, must lie between 1 and *MaxWorldsGlb* (as defined in the TYPEDEF.SYS file), and the *Low* coordinates must be lower in numeric value than their respective *Hi* coordinates; otherwise, an error will occur.

See Also   DefineWindow
            SelectWindow
            SelectWorld

Example   DefineWorld(1,0,-1,2*Pi,1);
            defines a world suitable for displaying one cycle of the sine function.

DisplayChar [GRAPHIX.SYS]

Declaration	**procedure** DisplayChar(C:byte);
Usage	DisplayChar(C);
Parameters	*C*: ASCII code of drawn character
Function	*DisplayChar* draws the character whose ASCII code is *C* at text coordinates [*XTextGlb,YTextGlb*] (internal variables). This procedure uses the font specific to the hardware configuration installed. *ConOutPtr* is set to point to this procedure while graphics mode is active.
Remarks	This procedure is for internal use by the graphics system. *XTextGlb* and *YTextGlb* are updated to the new cursor position.
Restrictions	None
See Also	DefineTextWindow TextDown TextLeft TextRight TextUp
Example	DisplayChar('!'); displays an exclamation point at the current cursor position, then advances the cursor.

DP [GRAPHIX.SYS]

Declaration	**procedure** DP(X,Y:integer);
Usage	DP(X,Y);
Parameters	*X,Y*: coordinates of drawn point
Function	*DP* draws a point at screen coordinates [*X,Y*].
Remarks	This procedure is primarily for internal use of the graphics system.
Restrictions	Since no clipping is performed by this procedure, it is important to specify valid *X* and *Y* parameters; otherwise, program memory may be encroached upon, or the system may crash.
See Also	DrawPoint
Example	DP(2,3);

    draws a point at screen coordinates [2,3] on the active screen in the current drawing color.

DrawAscii [KERNEL.SYS]

Declaration	**procedure** DrawAscii(Var X,Y:integer; Size,Ch:byte);
Usage	DrawAscii(X,Y,Size,Ch);
Parameters	*X,Y* : coordinates of drawn character *Size* : size of character *Ch* : ASCII value of character

Function

DrawAscii draws a single character with ASCII value *Ch* at screen coordinates [*X,Y*]. The 4x6-pixel character set is used. The character is drawn with its upper left corner at screen coordinates (*X,Y* − (2 × *Size*) + 1). Each point of the character is drawn as a *Size*-by-*Size* box, so the character is multiplied by *Size* in both directions. *X* is changed to *X* + (6 × *Size*), so that another call to *DrawAscii* using the same *X* and *Y* variables would draw the next character one position to the right (with a 2 × *Size* blank space between the characters).

Remarks

The character is clipped at the boundaries of the active window if clipping is enabled with *SetClippingOn*. The character would be displayed to the right, and both above and below coordinates [*X,Y*]

Restrictions

None

See Also

DefineHeader
DrawText
DrawTextW

Example

DrawAscii(20,40,25,'W');
draws a very large (100x150 pixel) *W* at screen coordinates [20,40]. Modifies *X* so that if another character of that size were drawn, it would be placed directly after the first character.

DrawAxis [AXIS.HGH]

Declaration	**procedure** DrawAxis(XDensity,YDensity,Left,Top,Right,Bottom: integer;XAxis,YAxis:integer;Arrows:boolean);

Usage
: DrawAxis(XDensity,YDensity,Left,Top,Right,Bottom,XAxis, YAxis,Arrows);

Parameters
: *XDensity* : density of tick marks on *X* ruler (− 9 to 9)
YDensity : density of tick marks on *Y* ruler (− 9 to 9)
Left   : distance of drawing area from left edge of window
Top   : distance of drawing area from top edge of window
Right   : distance of drawing area from right edge of window
Bottom : distance of drawing area from bottom edge of window
XAxis   : line style of horizontal axis
YAxis   : line style of vertical axis
Arrows : if TRUE, arrow symbols drawn at ends of axes; if FALSE, arrows not drawn

Function
: *DrawAxis* draws *X* and *Y* axes with ruler markings in the active window, to provide coordinate reference information for plots and drawings. This procedure can optionally define the world drawing area to be smaller than a window, draw a line around the drawing area, provide automatically labeled rulers for *X* and *Y* axes with variable tick mark density, and coordinate axes in various line styles.

The parameters *Left,Top, Right,* and *Bottom* move the drawing area in from the edges of the active window. If these parameters are all equal to 0, the drawing area is the entire window. *XDensity* and *YDensity* select how close together tick marks are drawn on the rulers, from -9 to 9. The sign of the *Density* parameters is ignored, except that if one of the *Density* parameters is negative and the other positive, a line is drawn around the drawing area. The *XAxis* and *YAxis* parameters specify the line styles of the horizontal and vertical axes. If either is negative in value, the corresponding axis is not drawn. The line styles correspond to those used to select line styles in the *DrawLine* procedure.

Restrictions   Moving the drawing area in from the edges of the active window is subject to the following conditions:

1. It only affects procedures *DrawHistogram* and *DrawPolygon*.
2. It is disabled after one call to either *DrawHistogram* or *DrawPolygon*.
3. To draw more polygons or histograms in this smaller window, set the global variable *AxisGlb* to TRUE before each additional call to *DrawPolygon* or *DrawHistogram*.

Example   DrawAxis(2,2,0,0,0,0,0,0,false);

draws solid axes that extend to the edges of the active window, with arrows on their ends. Numbers on the axes are displayed very far apart.

DrawAxis(9,-1,1,4,1,4,1,-1,true);

draws a dashed horizontal axis with an arrow on the end, and with numbers displayed very close together. Axis is drawn in an area that is smaller than the active window by 8 pixels on the right and left and 4 pixels on the top and bottom. A border is drawn around the drawing area.

DrawBorder [KERNEL.SYS]

Declaration	**procedure** DrawBorder;
Usage	DrawBorder;
Function	*DrawBorder* draws a border around the active window in the current drawing color and line style.
Remarks	If a header has been defined for the active window with the *DefineHeader* procedure, *DrawBorder* positions the header on the upper edge of the window if *SetHeaderToTop* has been called, or on the lower edge of the window if *SetHeaderToBottom* has been called. A header reduces the available drawing area in the window; if no header is defined, the whole window is used as the drawing area.
	DrawBorder does not erase the active window. If you need to erase the window background, use *SetBackground* (set to 0).
Restrictions	If the header is too long to fit within the window, it is not drawn. (Header length $\times$ 6) must be less than the width of the window in pixels, -2.
See Also	DefineHeader DrawSquare SetBackground SetHeaderOff SetHeaderOn SetHeaderToBottom SetHeaderToTop
Example	DrawBorder; draws a border around the active window, along with a header or footer if one was previously defined with the *DefineHeader* procedure.

DrawCartPie [PIE.HGH] (also requires CIRCSEGM.HGH)

Declaration	**procedure** DrawCartPie(XCenter,YCenter,XStart,YStart, Inner,Outer:real;A:PieArray; N,Option, Scale:integer;
Usage	DrawCartPie(XCenter,YCenter,XStart,YStart,Inner,Outer, A,N,Option,Scale);

Parameters

XCenter, YCenter	: world coordinates of center point of circle
XStart, YStart	: world coordinates of starting point of first circle segment
Inner	: inner radius of label line in radius units
Outer	: outer radius of label line in radius units
A	: pie chart array
N	: number of circle segments
Option	: labeling options
	Option = 0 : no label
	Option = 1 : text label only
	Option = 2 : text and numeric label
1	*Option* = 3 : numeric label only
Scale	: multiplier for specifying size of label

Data Format

Pie chart data is passed to the procedure as an array of the following form:

```
type PieType=record
             Area:real;
             Text:wrkstring;
    end;
PieArray=array [1..MaxPiesGlb] of PieType;
```

Function

DrawCartPie draws a pie chart, referenced to the *X* and *Y* coordinates of the starting point of the first pie segment, with optional text or numeric labels. Each segment's area and label are passed to the procedure in the *PieArray*, *A*, which defines the pie chart to be drawn.

DrawCartPie first determines each segment's proportion of the whole pie chart, then draws and labels the segments. Each segment's percentage of the pie chart is determined by totaling the areas of all segments, then displaying each segment's area as a percentage of the total area. Since this computation of percentage is not affected by the absolute values of the areas, any number system can be used for specifying the areas. A negative value for area causes the pie segment to move out radially and be displayed separately from the rest of the pie chart.

A line is drawn from each pie segment, starting at a distance of *Inner* away from the center segment and ending at a distance of *Outer*. A text and/or numeric label can be drawn at the end of each segment line in the 4x6-pixel character set. *Inner* and *Outer* specify the inner and outer radii that the radial label line is to traverse, with 1 being on the circle itself. *Option* specifies whether the area value and/or text is displayed; a value of 0 designates no label, 1 specifies text label only, 2, text and numeric label, and 3, numeric label only. *Scale* specifies the size of the characters that make up the label.

Remarks

Pie segments are drawn in a clockwise direction. Any part of the pie chart that lies outside the window boundaries is clipped if clipping is enabled with the *SetClippingOn* procedure.

Note that the aspect ratio is applied to pie charts. The aspect ratio must be set to 1 with the *SetAspect* procedure to ensure a circular pie chart.

To draw a pie chart with reference to its radius and the angle of its first segment, use *DrawPolarPie*.

See Also

DrawCircleSegment
DrawPolarPie
PieArray (type)
SetAspect

Example

DrawCartPie(100,100,125,100,1.1,1.4,SalesFigures,9,2,1);
draws a pie chart, with 9 sections, from the *SalesFigures* array. The starting point of the first pie segment is at [125,100]. Both numeric and text labels are attached to the pie with short lines. Labels are drawn in 4x6-pixel characters without scaling.

DrawCircle [KERNEL.SYS]

Declaration	**procedure** DrawCircle(X,Y,R:real);
Usage	DrawCircle(X,Y,R);
Parameters	*X,Y*: coordinates of point at center of circle or ellipse *R* : radius of circle or ellipse
Function	*DrawCircle* draws circles and ellipses. The circle or ellipse is drawn with its radius measured in the horizontal (*X*) direction, and with *Radius* × *Aspect* in the vertical (*Y*) direction.
Remarks	The horizontal-to-vertical ratio (aspect ratio) is set with the procedure *SetAspect*. Small aspects produce ellipses stretched horizontally, and large aspects produce vertical ellipses, while an aspect of 1 draws a true circle.
Restrictions	If *SetWindowModeOn* has been called, the value of the radius should be provided in an order of magnitude of 1; if *SetWindowModeOff* has been called, the order of magnitude should be 100.
See Also	AspectFactor (constant) DrawCircleDirect DrawCircleSegment SetAspect
Example	DrawCircle(20,40,15) draws a circle whose center point is at coordinates [20,40] with a radius of 15.

DrawCircleDirect [KERNEL.SYS]

Declaration	**procedure** DrawCircleDirect(X,Y,R:integer; Clip:boolean);
Usage	DrawCircleDirect(X,Y,R,Clip);
Parameters	*X,Y* : screen coordinates of point at center of circle or ellipse *R* : radius of circle or ellipse *Clip* : enables/disables clipping
Function	*DrawCircleDirect* draws a circle or ellipse, with the radius measured in *X* units of the screen. If *Clip* is TRUE, the circle is clipped at window boundaries; if FALSE, the circle is not clipped.
Remarks	This procedure is used for fast circle drawing. It should be used with caution, since it could cause drawing outside the physical screen. *DrawCircle* should be used in applications where speed of operations is not crucial.
Restrictions	None
See Also	DrawCircle SetAspect
Example	DrawCircleDirect(100,100,100,true); draws a circle at screen coordinates [100,100] with a radius of 100 pixels, without clipping at window boundaries.

DrawCircleSegment [CIRCSEGM.HGH]

Declaration **procedure** DrawCircleSegment(XCenter,YCenter:real;var XStart, YStart:real;Inner,Outer,Angle,Area:real;Text: WrkString;Option,Scale:byte);

Usage DrawCircleSegment(XCenter,YCenter,XStart,YStart,Inner, Outer,Angle,Area,Text,Option,Scale);

Parameters *XCenter, YCenter* : coordinates of point at center of circle
XStart, YStart : coordinates of starting point of segment
Inner : inner radius of label line in radius units
Outer : outer radius of label line in radius units
Angle : angle of segment in degrees
Area : numeric label corresponding to segment
Text : text label corresponding to segment
Option : display options
Option = 0 : no label
Option = 1 : text label only
Option = 2 : text and numeric label
Option = 3 : numeric label only
Scale : multiplier used to determine the size of label

Function *DrawCircleSegment* draws an arc of a circle with optional text and numeric labels. The center of the circle is at coordinates [*XCenter, YCenter*] (world coordinates), and the starting point of the arc is at coordinates [*XStart, YStart*]. The angle of the arc is passed directly in degrees. A line segment pointing outwards from the arc is drawn starting at a distance *Inner* away from the arc, and continuing to a distance *Outer*. After the segment is drawn, the coordinates of the endpoint are passed back through the starting position variables.

Text and/or numeric labels can be added. A radial label line can be drawn from the center of the circle segment outward to any location; its inside starting point is specified by *Inner* and its outside radius by *Outer*. *Inner* and *Outer* are scaled radius values: a value of 1 specifies a point on the circle segment, 0.5 a point halfway between the circle segment and its center, and a value of 2 indicates a point one radius distance outside the circle segment. A value of 1 for both inner and outer radii effectively disables the line so it does not appear. The outer radius determines where the label is to be placed. The *Option* parameter specifies whether to type text and/or numerics as the label; a value of 0 specifies no label, 1 specifies text label only, and 2, both text and numeric label. Labels are drawn in the 4x6-pixel character set. *Scale* determines the size of the characters in the label.

Remarks

If part of the segment lies outside the defined window boundaries and *SetClippingOn* has been called, the segment is clipped at window boundaries.

The aspect ratio is used by this procedure; see the *SetAspect* procedure.

Restrictions

If *Inner* or *Outer* is equal to 0, the label line is not drawn.

See Also

AspectFactor (constant)
DrawCartPie
DrawCircle
DrawCircleDirect
DrawPolarPie
SetAspect

Example

DrawCircleSegment(X,Y,ArcX,ArcY,1.1,1.4,30,2300,'Capital gains: $',2,1)

draws an arc starting at [*ArcX,ArcY*] that extends 30 degrees counterclockwise, centered around coordinates [*X,Y*]. A line is added with label saying *Capital gains: $2300* in 4x6-pixel characters.

DrawCross [KERNEL.SYS]

Declaration   **procedure** DrawCross(X,Y,Scale:integer);

Usage   DrawCross(X,Y,Scale);

Parameters   *X,Y* : coordinates of point at center of cross
                Scale : multiplier for specifying size of cross

Function   *DrawCross* draws a cross (+) at coordinates [*X,Y*]. The
                size of the cross is approximately 2**Scale* × 2**Scale*.

Remarks   This procedure is primarily for internal use of the graph-
                ics system; it is used by *DrawPolygon* to mark lines.

Restrictions   None

See Also   DrawCrossDiag
                DrawDiamond
                DrawStar
                DrawWye

Example   DrawCross(137,42,5);
                draws a cross at screen coordinates [137,42].

DrawCrossDiag [KERNEL.SYS]

Declaration	**procedure** DrawCrossDiag(X,Y,Scale:integer);
Usage	DrawCrossDiag(X,Y,Scale);
Parameters	*X,Y* : coordinates of point at center of cross *Scale* : multiplier for specifying size of cross
Function	*DrawCrossDiag* draws a diagonal cross (x) at coordinates [*X,Y*]. The size of the diagonal cross is approximately 2*Scale × 2*Scale.
Remarks	This procedure is primarily for internal use of the graphics system; it is used by *DrawPolygon* to mark lines.
Restrictions	None
See Also	DrawCross DrawDiamond DrawStar DrawWye
Example	DrawCrossDiag(89,70,8); draws a diagonal cross at screen coordinates [89,70].

DrawDiamond [KERNEL.SYS]

Declaration	**procedure** DrawDiamond(X,Y,Scale:integer);
Usage	DrawDiamond(X,Y,Scale);
Parameters	*X,Y* : coordinates of point at center of diamond *Scale* : multiplier for specifying size of diamond
Function	*DrawDiamond* draws a diamond (◇) at coordinates [*X,Y*]. The size of the diamond is approximately 2*Scale × 2*Scale.
Remarks	This procedure is primarily for internal use of the graphics system; it is used by *DrawPolygon* to mark lines.
Restrictions	None
Example	DrawDiamond(470,40,4); draws a diamond at screen coordinates [470,40].

DrawHistogram [HISTOGRM.HGH]

Declaration	**procedure** DrawHistogram(A:PlotArray; N:integer); Hatching:boolean; HatchStyle:integer);

Usage   DrawHistogram(A,N,Hatching,HatchStyle);

Parameters
     A   : array of bar chart
     N   : number of bars in chart
     Hatching   : enable or disable hatching
     HatchStyle : density of hatching
                       negative value = positive slope direction
                       positive value = negative slope direction

Data Format   Bar chart data is passed in an array of the type *Plot-Array*, with the following form:

$A[i,1]$ = not used
$A[i,2]$ = height of the i'th bar (Y value)

Function   *DrawHistogram* can create many types of bar charts with different hatchings and an optional axis display.

DrawHistogram draws a bar chart from an array, *A*, of real number values, [*MaxPlotGlb*,2]. *DrawHistogram* uses the [*i*,2] elements of the array to determine the height of each bar. The array is somewhat compatible with a polygon array, in that the *Y* axis components are displayed with constant increments in the *X* dimension. *DrawHistogram* calculates these increments from the window display width and the number of elements in the array to be displayed. The height of the histogram bars are scaled using the world coordinate system active at the time. The bars can be displayed in two modes: they can either be drawn from the bottom of the display area, or from the *Y* axis. When *N*, which specifies the number of bars in the chart, is positive, the bars are drawn from the bottom of the display area, and the absolute value function is applied. This forces all values to be positive, and thus prevents negative values from overwriting the ruler display when it is near the *Y* axis. When *N* is negative, bars are drawn from the *Y* axis, and the actual positive and negative values are used.

If *Hatching* is TRUE, each bar is hatched. The density and direction of the hatch lines is determined by *HatchStyle*. The value of *HatchStyle* determines the number of pixels between hatch lines; a value of 1 gives solid bars with no hatching, with increasing values widening the space between bars. The sign of the *HatchStyle* value determines the initial direction of hatching; hatching direction alternates with each consecutive bar. If *HatchStyle* is negative, the initial hatch line is drawn with a positive slope; if *HatchStyle* is positive, it is drawn with negative slope.

Remarks   The active window is entirely filled horizontally with the bar chart.

Restrictions   The number of bars is limited by the constant *MaxPlotGlb*, as defined in the TYPEDEF.SYS file.

See Also   MaxPlotGlb (constant)

Example   DrawHistogram(BarChartPoints,-40,true,6);
draws a bar chart with 40 bars in the active window. The bars may go up or down from the (invisible) horizontal axis, and they are hatched sparsely.

DrawLine [KERNEL.SYS]

Declaration	**procedure** DrawLine(X1,Y1,X2,Y2:real);
Usage	DrawLine(X1,Y1,X2,Y2);
Parameters	*X1,Y1* : coordinates of starting point of line *X2,Y2* : coordinates of end point of line
Function	*DrawLine* draws a line from [*X1,Y1*] to [*X2,Y2*] in the line style selected by the *SetLinestyle* procedure.
Remarks	The line is drawn in world coordinates unless the window mode is disabled with the *SetWindowModeOff* procedure, in which case the line is drawn in absolute screen coordinates. With window mode enabled, any part of the line that lies outside the window boundaries is clipped.
See Also	DrawStraight SetLinestyle
Restrictions	None
Example	DrawLine(40,107.5,99,50) draws a line between world coordinates [40,107.5] and [99,50].

DrawLineClipped [KERNEL.SYS]

Declaration	**procedure** DrawLineClipped(X1,Y1,X2,Y2:integer);
Usage	DrawLineClipped(X1,Y1,X2,Y2);
Parameters	*X1,Y1* : coordinates of starting point of line *X2,Y2* : coordinates of end point of line
Function	*DrawLineClipped* is a special procedure used to draw a line safely when the window mode is disabled with the *SetWindowModeOff* procedure. The line is drawn in absolute screen coordinates.
Remarks	This procedure clips a line at the active window boundaries, regardless of whether window mode is on or off.
Restrictions	None
See Also	DrawLine
Example	DrawLineClipped(1,1,199,199); draws a line between screen coordinates [1,1] and [199,199].

DrawPoint [KERNEL.SYS]

Declaration	**procedure** DrawPoint(X,Y:real);
Usage	DrawPoint(X,Y);
Parameters	*X,Y* : coordinates of point
Function	*DrawPoint* draws or redraws a point at coordinates [*X,Y*]. If window mode is enabled with the *SetWindowModeOn* procedure, the point is drawn in the active window in world coordinates and is scaled accordingly; if window mode is disabled with the *SetWindowModeOff* procedure, the point is drawn in absolute screen coordinates.
Remarks	If clipping is enabled with the *SetClippingOn* procedure, the point is clipped (not displayed) if it lies outside the active window boundaries.
See Also	SetColorBlack SetColorWhite
Restrictions	None
Example	DrawPoint(35.9,50.2) draws a point at world coordinates [35.9,50.2].

For Phi:=0 **To** 359 **Do**
DrawPoint(Phi,Sin(Phi*Pi/180));
draws one cycle of a sine wave, with the world coordinate system defined by coordinates [0, − 1] and [359,1].

DrawPolarPie [PIE.HGH] (requires CIRCSEGM.HGH)

Declaration	**procedure** DrawPolarPie(XCenter,YCenter,Radius,Angle, Inner,Outer:real;A:PieArray; N,Option, Scale:integer;
Usage	DrawPolarPie(XCenter,YCenter,Radius,Angle,Inner,Outer, A,N,Option,Scale);

Parameters

XCenter,YCenter	: world coordinates of center point of circle
Radius	: radius of pie
Angle	: angle of first pie segment (in degrees)
Inner	: inner radius of label line in radius units
Outer	: outer radius of label line in radius units
A	: pie chart array
N	: number of circle segments
Option	: labeling options
	Option = 0 : no label
	Option = 1 : text label only
	Option = 2 : text and numeric label
	Option = 3 : numeric label only
Scale	: multiplier for specifying size of label

Data Format Pie chart data is passed to the procedure as an array of the following form:

```
type PieType=record
          Area:real;
          Text:wrkstring;
     end;
     PieArray=array [1..MaxPiesGlb] of PieType;
```

Function

DrawPolarPie draws a pie chart, referenced to its radius and the angle of its first segment, with optional text or numeric labels. Each segment's area and label are passed to the procedure in the *PieArray, A*, which defines the pie chart to be drawn.

DrawPolarPie first determines each segment's proportion of the whole pie chart, then draws and labels the segments. Each segment's percentage of the pie chart is determined by totaling the areas of all segments, then displaying each segment's area as a percentage of the total area. Since this computation of percentage is not affected by the absolute values of the areas, any number system can be used for specifying the areas. A negative value for area causes the pie segment to move out radially and be displayed separately from the rest of the pie chart.

A line is drawn from each pie segment, starting at a distance of *Inner* away from the center segment and ending at a distance of *Outer*. A text and/or numeric label can be drawn at the end of each segment line in the 4x6-pixel character set. *Inner* and *Outer* specify the inner and outer radii that the radial label line is to traverse, with 1 being on the circle itself. *Option* specifies whether the area value and/or text is displayed; a value of 0 designates no label, 1 specifies text label only, and 2, text and numeric label. *Scale* specifies the size of the characters that make up the label.

Remarks

Pie segments are drawn in a clockwise direction. Any part of the pie chart that lies outside the window boundaries is clipped if clipping is enabled with the *SetClippingOn* procedure.

Note that the aspect ratio is applied to pie charts. The aspect ratio must be set to 1 with the *SetAspect* procedure to ensure a circular pie chart.

To draw a pie chart in reference to the starting point (*X* and *Y* coordinates) of its first segment, use *DrawCartPie*.

See Also

DrawCartPie
DrawCircleSegment
PieArray (type)
SetAspect

Example

DrawPolarPie(100,100,50,45,1.1,1.4,SalesFigures,9,2,1);
draws a pie chart, with 9 sections, from the *SalesFigures* array. Its radius is 50, and its first segment has a 45 degree angle. Both numeric and text labels are attached to the pie with short lines. Labels are drawn in 4x6-pixel characters without scaling.

DrawPolygon [POLYGON.HGH]

Declaration	**procedure** DrawPolygon(A:PlotArray; First,Last,Code,Scale, Lines:integer);
Usage	DrawPolygon(A,First,Last,Code,Scale,Lines);
Parameters	*A* : polygon vertex array (see data format) *First* : array index of first vertex to plot *Last* : array index of last vertex to plot *Code* : code of a graphic symbol *Scale* : multiplier for specifying size of symbol (scaling) *Lines* : choice of bar presentation

Data Format

The coordinates of the points of a polygon are passed in the global array *PlotArray*. The data type *PlotArray* is defined as follows:

type PlotArray = array [1..MaxPlotGlb,1..2] of real;

MaxPlotGlb is a constant that gives the maximum number of vertices (points) of a polygon. This number is preset to 100, but may be changed to any number by editing the TYPEDEF.SYS file.

The coordinates of the points must be presented in the following manner:

A[*i*,1] = *X* coordinate of the *i*th point
A[*i*,2] = *Y* coordinate of the *i*th point

Function

DrawPolygon draws a polygon using line segments with variable attributes and vertex symbols. The polygon is drawn in the active window in the current drawing color and line style.

First and *Last* define the range of the array, *A*. When *Last* is negative, all drawings are clipped. This is useful after rotations, moves, scaling, or after the world coordinate system has been changed. When *Last* is positive, only symbols are clipped, and drawing takes places faster than in the full clipping mode.

First specifies the array index of the first vertex to plot. If any of the following conditions are not fulfilled, an error occurs.

First < abs(*Last*)
First > 0
abs(*Last*) − *First* ≥ 2

Code specifies the code for a graphics symbol. If *Code* is a negative value, only symbols are displayed at vertices; if it is positive, symbols are displayed at vertices, and the vertices are connected with lines in the line style chosen by the *SetLinestyle* procedure. The following list shows the available symbols, along with their codes.

Code	Symbol
0	line
1	(+)
2	(X)
3	(□)
4	(■)
5	(◇)
6	(Y)
7	(*)
8	(O)
9	(.)
> 9	line

Scale determines the size of the symbol; its value must always be greater than 1.

Line determines whether or not vertical lines are drawn from the axis to the vertices. Options are:

Line < 0: lines are drawn from *Y*-zero-axis to each vertex

Line = 0: no lines

Line > 0: lines are drawn up from bottom of display area to each vertex

Remarks

To draw coordinate axes for the polygon, call *DrawAxis* before calling *DrawPolygon*.

Restrictions

None

See Also

PlotArray (type)

Example

DrawPolygon(Points,10,30,8,1,0);
    draws the 10th through 30th points of the *Points* array. Points are displayed as small circles, and are connected by lines drawn in the current line style.

DrawSquare [KERNEL.SYS]

Declaration	**procedure** DrawSquare(X1,Y1,X2,Y2:real; Fill:boolean);
Usage	DrawSquare(X1,Y1,X2,Y2,Fill);
Parameters	*X1,Y1* : world coordinates of point at upper left corner of rectangle *X2,Y2* : world coordinates of point at lower right corner of rectangle *Fill* : enables/disables filling of rectangle
Function	*DrawSquare* draws a rectangle, with point [*X1,Y1*] as the upper left corner and point [*X2,Y2*] as the lower right corner. The rectangle is drawn in the line style selected by the *SetLineStyle* procedure. When *Fill* is TRUE, the rectangle is filled with the current drawing color.
Remarks	To fill a square with a background pattern, define the square as a window and use *SetBackground* or *SetBackground8*.
Restrictions	None
See Also	DrawLine DrawStraight SetForegroundColor SetLinestyle
Example	

DrawSquare(2,3,50,90,true);
    draws a solid rectangle defined by world coordinates [2,3] through [50,90}

DrawSquareC [KERNEL.SYS]

Declaration	**procedure** DrawSquareC(X1,Y1,X2,Y2:integer; Fill:boolean);

Parameters   *X1,Y1* : screen coordinates of point at upper left corner
of rectangle
X2,Y2 : screen coordinates of point at lower right corner
of rectangle
Fill   : enables/disables filling of rectangle

Function   *DrawSquareC* draws a rectangle, with coordinate
[*X1,Y1*] at the upper left corner and coordinate [*X2,Y2*]
at the lower right corner of the rectangle. The rectangle
is drawn in screen coordinates, but is clipped at the
boundaries of the active window.

Remarks   This procedure is used internally by the *DrawBorder* procedure.

Restrictions   None

See Also   DrawSquare

Example   DrawSquareC(2,3,50,90,false);
draws the part of the square (defined by screen coordinates [2,3] and [50,90]) that fits in the active window.

DrawStar [KERNEL.SYS]

Declaration   **procedure** DrawStar(X,Y,Scale:integer);

Usage   DrawStar(X,Y,Scale);

Parameters   *X,Y* : coordinates of center point of star
               Scale : multiplier for determining size of star

Function   *DrawStar* draws a six-pointed star (*) at coordinates
               [*X,Y*]. The size of the star is approximately 2*Scale* ×
               2*Scale* (in pixels).

Remarks   This procedure is mainly for internal use by the graphics
               system; it is used by *DrawPolygon* for marking lines.

Restrictions   None

See Also   DrawCross
                DrawCrossDiag
                DrawDiamond
                DrawWye

Example   DrawStar(400,130,30);
                   draws a large star at screen coordinates [400,130].

DrawStraight [GRAPHIX.SYS]

Declaration   **procedure** DrawStraight(X1,X2,Y:integer);

Usage   DrawStraight(X1,X2,Y);

Parameters   *X1* :*X* screen coordinate of starting point of line
X2 :*X* screen coordinate of end point of line
Y :*Y* screen coordinate of line

Function   *DrawStraight* draws a horizontal line from [*X1,Y*] to [*X2,Y*] in absolute screen coordinates; no clipping is performed.

Remarks   Although *DrawLine* can accomplish the same function as *DrawStraight*, this procedure performs the task of drawing horizontal lines much faster. *DrawStraight* is useful for speedy filling of squares. The line is always drawn in line style 0 (See *SetLinestyle*).

Restrictions   None

See Also   DrawLine
SetLinestyle

Example   DrawStraight(23,502,100);
draws a long horizontal line between screen coordinates [23,100] and [502,100].

DrawText [KERNEL.SYS]

Declaration   **procedure** DrawText(X,Y,Scale:integer; Text:WrkString);

Usage   DrawText(X,Y,Scale,Text);

Parameters   *X,Y* : coordinates of point at beginning of character string
               Scale : multiplier for specifying character size
               Text : character string

Function   *DrawText* draws the given string, *Text*, beginning at
               screen coordinates [*X,Y*]. The procedure uses the 4x6-
               pixel character set multiplied both vertically and horizon-
               tally by *Scale*. If an ESCape (character 27 decimal) is in
               the string, a particular symbol is drawn according to the
               next character in the string.

               There are eight possible symbols, corresponding to the
               sequences ESC 1 through ESC 8:

               1 = +
               2 = ×
               3 = □
               4 = ■
               5 = ◇
               6 = 'Y'
               7 = *
               8 = O

               The symbols are drawn to the same scale as the text.
               The ESCape sequence can also be given in the form
               ESC *n* @ *s*, where *n* is a number between 1 and 8 and *s*
               is an integer value. In this case, ESC *n* designates which
               symbol to draw, while *s* specifies the scale of the sym-
               bol. For instance, the sequence ESC 1 @ 5 would draw
               a cross with a scale of 5.

Remarks   Text is clipped at active window boundaries if *SetClip-
               pingOn* has been called.

Restrictions   None

See Also   DrawTextW

Example

```
DrawText(100,100,2,'Some text');
```
draws the character string *Some text* beginning at screen coordinates [100,100], in 8x12-pixel characters.

```
DrawText(250,19,3,'This is a diamond: '+Chr(27)+'5';
```
draws the character string *This is a diamond* ◇ beginning at screen coordinates [250,19] in 12x18-pixel characters.

DrawTextW

Declaration	**procedure** DrawTextW(X,Y,Scale:real; Text:WrkString);
Usage	DrawTextW(X,Y,Scale,Text);
Parameters	*X,Y* : world coordinates of point at beginning of character string *Scale* : multiplier for specifying character size *Text* : character string
Function	*DrawTextW* draws the given string, beginning at world coordinates [*X,Y*]. The procedure uses the 4x6-pixel character set multiplied both vertically and horizontally by *Scale*. If an ESCape (character 27 decimal) is in the string, a particular symbol is drawn according to the next character in the string.
Remarks	See *DrawText* for possible ESC sequence symbols.
Restrictions	None
See Also	DisplayChar DrawText
Example	DrawTextW(5.7,19.02,3,'This text starts at (5.7,19.02) in world coordinates'); draws the character string beginning at world coordinates (5.7,19.02) in the active window.

DrawWye [KERNEL.SYS]

Declaration   **procedure** DrawWye(X,Y,Scale:integer);

Usage   DrawWye(X,Y,Scale);

Parameters   *X,Y* : coordinates of center point of *Y* symbol
                  Scale : multiplier for specifying size of symbol

Function   *DrawWye* draws a Y-shaped symbol at coordinates
                  [*X,Y*]. The size of the *Y* is approximately 2*Scale ×
                  2*Scale.

Remarks   This procedure is mainly for internal use by the graphics
                  system; it is used by *DrawPolygon* for marking lines.

Restrictions   None

See Also   DrawCross
                  DrawCrossDiag
                  DrawDiamond
                  DrawStar

Example   DrawWye(50,90,4);
                  draws a *Y*-shaped figure at screen coordinates [50,90].

EnterGraphic [GRAPHIX.SYS]

Declaration   **procedure** EnterGraphic;

Usage   EnterGraphic;

Function   *EnterGraphic* turns the graphics mode on and clears the screen. This procedure is normally called to reactivate the graphics mode after *LeaveGraphic* has been called.

Remarks   *EnterGraphic* does not initialize the graphics system; to do that, *InitGraphic* must be called. *EnterGraphic* also loads the system-dependent (higher quality) character set the first time it is called, and sets *ConOutPtr* to point to *DisplayChar*.

After *EnterGraphic* is called, "black" will be true black and "white" will be true white, regardless of the graphics card installed. A call to *SetBackgroundColor* or *SetForegroundColor*, followed by a call to *EnterGraphic*, will cancel the colors set by the *SetColor* procedures and set them to true black and white.

Restrictions   None

See Also   InitGraphic
LeaveGraphic

Example   EnterGraphic;
clears the screen, sets the colors to true black and white, and turns graphics mode on.

Error [KERNEL.SYS]

Declaration	**procedure** Error(Proc,Code);
Usage	Error(Proc,Code);
Parameters	*Proc* : address of procedure where error was detected *Code* : error code

Function

Error is called when an error is discovered by one of the Turbo Graphix procedures; the address of the procedure and an error code are given. If break mode is enabled with the *SetBreakOn* procedure, an error will halt the program and an error message and a trace of the addresses of the procedures in the calling sequence that caused the error are displayed. If break mode is disabled with the *SetBreakOff* procedure, the *Error* procedure stores the error code for later examination when the *GetErrorCode* function is called. If message mode is enabled with the *SetMessageOn* procedure, a message is displayed, regardless of *SetBreakOn/Off*.

Remarks

Error messages are displayed on line 25 of the screen. If *SetBreakOn* has been called, a list of addresses is displayed. The first address given is the location of the call to *Error*. If the compiler *Option Find* is used on the program, the compiler will display the statement *Error(p,c)* for the graphics procedure where the error was detected. The next number is the address of the statement that called the procedure that found the error. Each successive number is the caller of the previous procedure. The last number points out the line in the main program that started the fatal calling sequence.

Restrictions

None

See Also

GetErrorCode
SetBreakOff
SetBreakOn
SetMessageOff
SetMessageOn

Example

Error(2,3);
    signals error code 3 in procedure 2.

FindWorld [FINDWRLD.HGH]

Declaration	**procedure** FindWorld(I:integer; A:PlotArray; N:integer; ScaleX,ScaleY:real);

Usage   FindWorld (I,A,N,ScaleX,ScaleY);

Parameters
I   : index of world
A   : polygon array
N   : number of vertices in polygon array
ScaleX : additional scaling factor in *X* direction
ScaleY : additional scaling factor in *Y* direction

Function
FindWorld determines a world coordinate system for a polygon. The procedure finds the maximum and minimum *X* and *Y* values used to draw a polygon, and then defines a world that either exactly encloses the polygon, or that is larger or smaller by some chosen percentage (*ScaleX* and *ScaleY*). *FindWorld* automatically executes *DefineWorld* and *SelectWorld* procedures after it determines the appropriate world coordinate system.

The *I* parameter selects the index of the world that is to be modified. The selected polygon, *A*, is passed in the *PlotArray*, with *N* specifying the number of vertices in the polygon. The *X* and *Y* dimensions can be multipled by *ScaleX* and *ScaleY*, respectively, to adjust the scaling of the world dimensions; this allows extra space around the polygon or changes its proportions. If no extra scaling is desired, *ScaleX* and *ScaleY* should be set to 1.

Remarks
For a more complete description of the data structure for polygons of the type *PlotArray*, refer to the description for *DrawPolygon*.

Restrictions   None

See Also
DefineWorld
DrawPolygon
PlotArray (type)
SelectWorld

Example
FindWorld(1,Diagram,30,1,2);
   sets a world coordinate system 1, so that the 30-point polygon *Diagram* exactly fits the world horizontally, and half fills it vertically.

GetAspect [KERNEL.SYS]

Declaration   **function** GetAspect:real;

Usage   GetAspect;

Function   *GetAspect* returns the current value of the aspect ratio.

Remarks   See *SetAspect* for complete information on the aspect ratio.

See Also   AspectFactor (constant)
               GetScreenAspect
               SetAspect
               SetScreenAspect

Restrictions   None

Example   R:=GetAspect;
               R gets the current aspect ratio.

GetColor [KERNEL.SYS]

Declaration	**function** GetColor:integer;
Usage	GetColor;
Function	*GetColor* returns the drawing color: 0 if the current color is "black", and 255 if it is "white".
Remarks	"Black" and "white" can be any color available to the particular graphics card installed. For more information on hardware configuration, see Chapter 1 and Appendix A.
See Also	SetBackgroundColor SetColorBlack SetColorWhite SetForegroundColor
Restrictions	None
Example	I:=GetColor; *I* is 0 if the current drawing color is black, or 255 if the current drawing color is white.

GetErrorCode [KERNEL.SYS]

Declaration   **function** GetErrorCode:integer;

Usage   GetErrorCode;

Function   *GetErrorCode* returns the error code of the most recent error, or − 1 if no error occurred. A call to *GetErrorCode* resets the error code to − 1.

The error codes are:
− 1 : No error
  0 : Error msg missing
  1 : Font file missing
  2 : Index out of range
  3 : Coordinates out of range
  4 : Too few array elements
  5 : Error opening file
  6 : Out of window memory
  7 : Value(s) out of range

Remarks   *GetErrorCode* should be called after the use of any routine that could cause the errors listed above.

Restrictions   The procedure or function that caused the error cannot be determined with this routine; see *SetBreakOn*.

See Also
Error
SetBreakOff
SetBreakOn
SetMessageOff
SetMessageOn

Example   **If** GetErrorCode < >−1 **Then** ShutDown;
executes procedure *ShutDown* if any graphics error has occurred.

GetLineStyle [KERNEL.SYS]

Declaration   **function** GetLineStyle:integer;

Usage   GetLineStyle;

Function   *GetLineStyle* returns the current line style (selected by *SetLineStyle*), an integer from 0 to 4, or 256 to 511.

Restrictions   None

See Also   SetLineStyle

Example   I:=GetLineStyle;
     I gets a value in the ranges 0..4 and 256..511, representing the current line style.

GetScreen [KERNEL.SYS]

Declaration   **function** GetScreen:integer;

Usage   GetScreen;

Function   *GetScreen* returns the code corresponding to the RAM
                (virtual) or displayed screen currently in use (active): code
                1 if the displayed screen is active, or 2 if the RAM screen
                is active.

Restrictions   None

See Also   SelectScreen

Example   I:=GetScreen;
                I is 1 if the displayed screen is the active screen, or 2 if
                the RAM screen is active.

GetScreenAspect [KERNEL.SYS]

Declaration   **function** GetAspect:real;

Usage   GetScreenAspect;

Function   *GetScreenAspect* returns the current pixel value of the aspect ratio.

Remarks   See *SetAspect* for complete information on the aspect ratio.

See Also   AspectFactor (constant)
               GetAspect
               SetAspect
               SetScreenAspect

Restrictions   None

Example   R:=GetScreenAspect;
               R gets the current aspect ratio, in pixels.

GetVStep [KERNEL.SYS]

Declaration **function** GetVStep:integer;

Usage GetVStep;

Function *GetVStep* returns the current value of the step (single increment) for vertical window movement.

Remarks See *SetVStep* for explanation of *step*.

Restrictions None

See Also SetVStep

Example I:=GetVStep;
I is the current vertical step value.

GetWindow [KERNEL.SYS]

Declaration	**function** GetWindow:integer;
Usage	GetWindow;
Function	*GetWindow* returns the code number of the active window (selected by *SelectWindow*).
Restrictions	None
See Also	SelectWindow
Example	I:=GetWindow; *I* is the code number of the active window.

GotoXY [KERNEL.SYS]

Declaration	**procedure** GotoXY(X,Y:integer);
Usage	GotoXY(X,Y);
Parameters	*X,Y*: coordinates of character
Function	*GotoXY* positions the text cursor (invisible cursor that determines where next character is to be drawn) at coordinates [*X,Y*].
Remarks	This procedure tells *DisplayChar* where to draw the next character, and thereby augments Turbo's normal *GotoXY* procedure.
Restrictions	None
See Also	DisplayChar GotoXYTurbo
Example	GotoXY(1,20); causes the cursor to be positioned at the first character on screen line 20.

GotoXYTurbo [KERNEL.SYS]

Declaration	**procedure** GotoXYTurbo(X,Y:integer);
Usage	GotoXYTurbo(X,Y);
Parameters	*X,Y* : coordinates of character
Function	*GotoXYTurbo* calls Turbo's *GotoXY* procedure, and aids the *DisplayChar* procedure by keeping track of the location of the *X* and *Y* coordinates of characters.
Remarks	This is an internal procedure.
Restrictions	None
See Also	DisplayChar GotoXY
Example	GotoXYTurbo(1,20);

causes the cursor to be positioned at the first character of screen line 20; however, the graphics system is unaware of the cursor.

HardCopy [KERNEL.SYS]

Declaration	**procedure** HardCopy(Inverse:boolean; Mode:byte);
Usage	HardCopy(Inverse,Mode);
Parameters	*Inverse* : enables/disables reverse video printout *Mode* : specifies print mode

Function
: *HardCopy* supplies a printed copy of the active screen. If *Inverse* is TRUE, the image is printed with black and white reversed. *Mode* specifies the density of the printed image. Seven modes are available:

$$
\begin{array}{lll}
0,4,5 & = & 640 \text{ points/line (Epson mode 4)} \\
1 & = & 960 \text{ points/line (Epson mode 1)} \\
2 & = & 960 \text{ points/line (Epson mode 2)} \\
3 & = & 1920 \text{ points/line (Epson mode 3)} \\
6 & = & 720 \text{ points/line (Epson mode 6)}
\end{array}
$$

Remarks
: This procedure can be used with Epson printers of series MX, RX, and FX. Pre-FX series printers can be used, but with Mode 1 only. See the Epson printer manuals for more information.

Restrictions
: Non-Epson printers are not supported.

See Also
: Epson printer manuals
SelectScreen

Example
: HardCopy(false,3);
    causes the active screen to be printed in Epson graphics mode 3.

HardwarePresent [GRAPHIX.SYS]

Declaration	**function** HardwarePresent:boolean;
Usage	HardwarePresent;
Function	*HardwarePresent* checks whether or not the necessary graphics hardware is installed in the system (i.e., IBM Color graphics adapter for IBM version, Hercules card for Hercules version) and returns TRUE if found. If *HardwarePresent* is FALSE, an error occurs.
Remarks	This is an internal function called by *InitGraphic*.
	This function is useful in a program that uses graphics mode only for certain presentations. If *HardwarePresent* is FALSE, those graphic presentations are not available.
Restrictions	If *InitGraphic* is called when *HardwarePresent* is FALSE, the program is terminated.
See Also	InitGraphic
| Example | ```
If Not HardwarePresent Then
  WriteLn('No graphics board detected in your computer.  Make
  another selection');
Else
  Begin
  {Do Graphics}
End;
``` |
```

Hatch [HATCH.HGH]

Declaration	**procedure** Hatch(X1,Y1,X2,Y2:real;Delta:integer);
Usage	Hatch(X1,Y1,X2,Y2,Delta);
Parameters	*X1,Y1* : coordinates of point at upper left corner of rectangle to be hatched *X2,Y2* : coordinates of point at lower right corner of rectangle to be hatched *Delta* : distance between hatch lines
Function	*Hatch* shades a rectangular area of the screen defined by world coordinates [*X1,Y1*] and [*X2,Y2*]. The hatch pattern is formed with diagonal lines separated by a distance of *Delta*. A *Delta* value of 1 gives solid hatching (no space between lines), a *Delta* value of 2 gives 50% filled space, a value of 3 gives 33⅓% filled space, and so on. If *Delta* is positive, the lines are drawn from the upper left to the lower right; if *Delta* is negative, the lines are drawn from the lower left to the upper right.
Remarks	If window mode is disabled with the *SetWindowModeOff* procedure, the rectangle is drawn in absolute screen coordinates.
Restrictions	None
See Also	DrawSquare
Example	Hatch(5,5,30,17,4); hatches part of the active window, defined by coordinates [5,5] and [30,17], with diagonal lines that fill ¼ of the given area.

InitGraphic [KERNEL.SYS]

Declaration	**procedure** InitGraphic;
Usage	InitGraphic;
Function	*InitGraphic* initializes the Turbo Graphix Toolbox. It must be called before any other graphics procedure or function, but may only be called once within a program. *InitGraphic* selects the displayed screen as the active screen and erases it. All windows and worlds are initialized. In addition, *InitGraphic* performs these functions:

- Checks for the presence of appropriate graphics hardware
- Reads in the error messages file
- Reads in the 4x6-pixel character set
- Allocates the RAM screen if *RamScreenGlb* is TRUE in the TYPEDEF.SYS file
- Sets aspect ratio to machine-dependent default
- Sets vertical window move step (increment) to machine-dependent default

InitGraphic calls the following procedures:

```
EnterGraphic;
HardwarePresent;
SelectWindow (1);
SelectWorld (1);
SelectScreen (1);
SetAspect (AspectFactor);
SetBackgroundColor (MinBackground);
SetBreakOn;
SetClippingOn;
SetColorWhite;
SetForegroundColor (MaxForeground);
SetHeaderOff;
SetHeaderToTop;
SetLineStyle (0);
SetMessageOn;
SetWindowModeOn;
```

Restrictions   *InitGraphic* can be called only once within a program.

See Also   EnterGraphic
LeaveGraphic

Example   `InitGraphic;`
initializes the graphics system and turns on graphics mode.

InvertScreen [GRAPHIX.SYS]

Declaration	**procedure** InvertScreen;
Usage	InvertScreen;
Function	*InvertScreen* inverts the screen display by changing pixels from black to white or white to black.
Remarks	"Black" and "white" can be any color available to the particular graphics card installed in your system. See Chapter 1 and Appendix A for more information on hardware configuration.
Restrictions	None
See Also	InvertWindow
Example	InvertScreen;

    changes each pixel on the active screen from "black" to "white", or from "white" to "black."

InvertWindow [WINDOWS.SYS]

Declaration   **procedure** InvertWindow;

Usage   InvertWindow;

Function   *InvertWindow* inverts the active window display by changing pixels from black to white or white to black.

Remarks   "Black" and "white" can be any color available to the particular graphics card installed in your system. See Chapter 1 and Appendix A for more information on hardware configuration.

Restrictions   None

See Also   InvertScreen

Example   InvertWindow;
     changes each pixel on the active window from "black" to "white," or from "white" to "black."

LeaveGraphic [GRAPHIX.SYS]

Declaration	**procedure** LeaveGraphic;
Usage	LeaveGraphic;
Function	*LeaveGraphic* turns the graphics mode off and returns the system to text mode (which was active before *InitGraphic* was called). *LeaveGraphic* also sets *ConOutPtr* back to its previous value.
Restrictions	None
See Also	EnterGraphic InitGraphic
Example	LeaveGraphic; turns graphics mode off and text mode on.

LoadScreen [GRAPHIX.SYS]

Declaration	**procedure** LoadScreen(FileName:WrkString);
Usage	LoadScreen(FileName);
Parameters	*FileName*: screen file name (as saved on disk)
Function	*LoadScreen* opens the file containing a graphics screen, named *FileName*, and reads the screen onto the active RAM or displayed screen.
Restrictions	Screens saved with one version of the Turbo Graphix Toolbox are not necessarily compatible with any other version. See Appendix A for more on system compatibility.
See Also	SaveScreen StoreScreen
Example	LoadScreen('SCREEN.1');

loads the contents of the file *SCREEN.1* into the active screen.

LoadWindow [WINDOWS.SYS]

Declaration	**procedure** LoadWindow(I,X,Y:integer; FileName:WrkString);
Usage	LoadWindow(I,X,Y,FileName);

Parameters   *I*   : index of window to be loaded
                     X,Y   : world coordinates of point where window is
                                       loaded
                     FileName : window file name (as stored on disk)

Function   *LoadWindow* loads a window, *I*, named by *FileName*, to position [*X,Y*] (world coordinates). If *X* or *Y* is negative, the previous (saved) *X* or *Y* coordinate value is used (i.e., the negative value is ignored.) The window is loaded into the active window, thereby erasing the contents of the old window.

Remarks   *FileName* can include both the filename and an extension, and a disk drive declaration (e.g., *b: filename.xxx*). Windows saved with different versions of the Turbo Graphix Toolbox are compatible. However, this is not the case for the *LoadScreen* procedure.

Restrictions   If a negative value is given for *X* or *Y*, the previous (saved) value for that coordinate is used.

See Also   LoadScreen
                     SaveScreen
                     SaveWindow

Example   LoadWindow(3,-1,20,'WINDOW.3');
                     loads the contents of the file *WINDOW.3* into window 3, using the *X* position previously stored in the file, and the new *Y* position (20).

LoadWindowStack [WINDOWS.SYS]

Declaration **procedure** LoadWindowStack(FileName:WrkString);

Usage LoadWindowStack(FileName);

Parameters *FileName*: filename of window stack (as stored on disk)

Function *LoadWindowStack* stores a window stack, named *FileName*, from disk to window memory. This procedure automatically searches for two files, *FileName.STK* (file containing the stack) and *FileName.PTR* (a pointer file); therefore, you should not add an extension to *FileName*.

Remarks When loading a window stack from a floppy or hard disk, the entire contents of the existing window stack are destroyed.

Restrictions Window stacks saved by different versions of the Turbo Graphix Toolbox will not necessarily be compatible. See Appendix A for more information on compatibility between systems.

See Also LoadWindow
SaveWindow
SaveWindowStack

Example LoadWindowStack('STACK');
loads a window stack from the files *STACK.STK* and *STACK.PTR*.

MoveHor [WINDOWS.SYS]

Declaration   **procedure** MoveHor(Delta:integer; FillOut:boolean);

Usage   MoveHor(Delta,FillOut);

Parameters   *Delta* : distance window is moved
FillOut: enable/disable copy from RAM screen

Function   *MoveHor* moves the active window horizontally by *Delta* steps (8 pixels per step). If *FillOut* is FALSE, the area that used to be under the window is filled with the opposite of the current color; if *FillOut* is TRUE, and there is a RAM screen allocated (*RamScreenGlb* is TRUE in TYPEDEF.SYS), the area is filled with the corresponding area of the inactive screen. Thus, to move a window over a background, the background must be stored in the inactive screen (with *CopyScreen*) before the window to be moved is drawn on the active screen. The background is then copied from the inactive screen as the window moves.

Restrictions   None

See Also   MoveVer
SetBackground

Example   MoveHor(-7,false);
moves the active window by 7 *X* window definition coordinates (56 pixels) to the left, filling the former location of the window with the opposite of the current drawing color.

MoveVer [WINDOWS.SYS]

Declaration	**procedure** MoveVer(Delta:integer; FillOut:boolean);
Usage	MoveVer(Delta,FillOut);
Parameters	*Delta* : distance window is moved *FillOut* : enable/disable copy from RAM screen
Function	*MoveVer* moves the current window vertically by *Delta* steps (1 pixel per step). If *FillOut* is FALSE, the area that used to be under the window is filled with the opposite of the current color; if *FillOut* is TRUE, and there is a RAM screen allocated (*RamScreenGlb* is TRUE in TYPEDEF.SYS file), the area is filled with the corresponding area of the inactive screen. Thus, to move a window over a background, the background must be stored to the inactive screen (with *CopyScreen*) before the window to be moved is drawn on the active screen. The background is then copied from the inactive screen as the window moves.
Remarks	*SetVStep* can be called to specify the number of pixels to move a window vertically at one time; this will speed the vertical movement of the window. For example, if *Delta* is 10 and *VStep* is 3, the window will move 3 times by 3, then once by 1, for a total move of 10 pixels (in the time a 4-pixel move would take without the use of *SetVStep*).
Restrictions	None
See Also	MoveHor
Example	MoveVer(20,true); moves the active window 20 pixels toward the bottom of the screen, filling the former location of the window with the contents of the same location on the inactive screen.

PD [GRAPHIX.SYS]

Declaration	**function** PD(X,Y):boolean;
Usage	PD(X,Y);
Parameters	*X,Y*: screen coordinates of point
Function	*PD* checks whether a point has been drawn at screen coordinates [*X,Y*]. *PD* returns TRUE if a point exists at [*X,Y*] in the current drawing color; otherwise, it returns FALSE.
Restrictions	None
See Also	DrawPoint PointDrawn
Example	B:=PD(5,5); *B* is TRUE if the point at screen coordinates [5,5] is set to the current drawing color.

```
PointCount:=0
For X:=0 To XScreenMaxGlb Do
  For Y:=0 To YMaxGlb Do
    If PD(X,Y) Then PointCount:=PointCount+1;
```
This program counts the number of points on the screen.

PointDrawn [GRAPHIX.SYS]

Declaration	**function** PointDrawn(X,Y):boolean;
Usage	PointDrawn(X,Y);
Parameters	*X,Y*: world coordinates of point
Function	*PointDrawn* checks whether or not a point has been drawn at world coordinates [*X,Y*]. *PointDrawn* returns TRUE if a point exists at [*X,Y*] in the current drawing color; otherwise, it returns FALSE.
Restrictions	None
See Also	DrawPoint PD
Example	B:=PointDrawn (12.3,17.8) *B* is TRUE if the point at world coordinates [12.3,17.8] is set in the current drawing color.

RedefineWindow [KERNEL.SYS]

Declaration	**procedure** RedefineWindow(I,XLow,YLow,XHi,YHi:integer);
Usage	RedefineWindow(I,XLow,XHi,YHi);
Parameters	*I* : index of window [1..*MaxWindowsGlb*] *XLow* : *X* value of upper left window position [0..*XMaxGlb*] *YLow* : *Y* value of upper left window position [0..*YMaxGlb*] *XHi* : *X* value of lower right window position [1..*XMaxGlb*] *YHi* : *Y* value of lower right window position [0..*YMaxGlb*]
Function	*RedefineWindow* redefines the dimensions of an existing window, *I*. The window is defined as a rectangle with the upper left corner at [*XLow,YLow*] and the lower right corner at [*XHi,YHi*]. The previously defined window header is not affected by *RedefineWindow*.
Remarks	The *X* coordinates of a window are defined in 8-pixel chunks; i.e, windows are placed on byte boundaries in memory. If *RedefineWindow* is called with parameters (1,10,10,19,19), the defined window is 10 pixels tall and 80 pixels wide.
Restrictions	The value of *I* must be between 1 and *MaxWindowsGlb* (as defined in the TYPEDEF.SYS file), all coordinates must lie within the physical screen, and the *Low* coordinates must be lower in numeric value than the *Hi* coordinates; otherwise, an error will occur.
See Also	DefineWindow SelectWindow

Example	RedefineWindow(4,5,5,10,10);
	    redefines window 4 , with upper left corner at window definition coordinates [5,5] and lower right corner at [10,10] (screen coordinates [40,5] and [87,10]).
	
	RedefineWindow(2,0,0,XMaxGlb div 2,YMaxGlb div 2);
	    redefines window 2 as the upper left quarter of the screen.

RemoveHeader [KERNEL.SYS]

Declaration   **procedure** RemoveHeader(I:integer);

Usage   RemoveHeader(I);

Parameters   *I* : index for window

Function   *RemoveHeader* removes the header from window *I*. As with *DefineHeader*, this procedure has no effect on the display of the header; the header is erased only when *DrawBorder* is called again.

Remarks   Once the header is removed, the drawing area of the window will include the part of the window that had been occupied by the header.

Restrictions   None

See Also   DefineHeader
DrawBorder
SetHeaderOn
SetHeaderToBottom
SetHeaderToTop

Example   RemoveHeader(8);
      removes the header of window 8, so that a subsequent call to *DrawBorder* will not draw the header.

ResetWindowStack [WINDOWS.SYS]

Declaration   **procedure** ResetWindowStack;

Usage   ResetWindowStack;

Function   *ResetWindowStack* erases all windows contained in memory. All windows saved in the window stack are discarded, and all the space allocated for the window stack becomes available for the storage of new windows.

Remarks   This procedure initializes the window stack in the same way as *InitGraphic*. It is especially useful for long programs that require several different drawing environments.

                  Windows saved in the window stack are dynamically allocated with Turbo Pascal's *GetMem* and *FreeMem* procedures. Because of this, the Mark/Release method of memory management must not be used.

Restrictions   None

See Also   InitGraphic
                  ResetWindows
                  ResetWorlds
                  RestoreWindow
                  StoreWindow

Example   ResetWindowStack;
                     discards any windows saved on the window stack.

ResetWindows [KERNEL.SYS]

Declaration   **procedure** ResetWindows;

Usage   ResetWindows;

Function   *ResetWindows* sets all windows to the size of the screen, selects Window 1 (see the *SelectWindow* procedure), and removes all headers. This procedure does not affect the current screen display, but further drawings will be scaled according to absolute screen coordinates.

Remarks   This procedure resets windows in the same way as *InitGraphic*.

Restrictions   None

See Also   InitGraphic
ResetWindowStack
ResetWorlds
SelectWindow

Example   ResetWindows;
sets all windows to the size of the screen.

ResetWorlds [KERNEL.SYS]

Declaration	**procedure** ResetWorlds;
Usage	ResetWorlds;
Function	*ResetWorlds* sets all worlds to the size of the physical screen and selects World 1. (See the *SelectWorld* procedure.) Further drawings will be scaled to absolute screen coordinates.
Remarks	This procedure resets worlds in the same way as *InitGraphic*.
Restrictions	None
See Also	InitGraphic ResetWindows ResetWindowStack SelectWorld
Example	ResetWorlds; sets all worlds to the size of the screen.

RestoreWindow [WINDOWS.SYS]

Declaration   **procedure** RestoreWindow(I,DeltaX,DeltaY:integer);

Usage   RestoreWindow(I,DeltaX,DeltaY);

Parameters   *I*   : index of window [1..*MaxWindowsGlb*]
               DeltaX : *X* offset
               DeltaY : *Y* offset

Function   *RestoreWindow* takes a window, *I*, that was stored in
               the window stack with the *StoreWindow* procedure and
               places it on the screen. If *I* is negative, the restored win-
               dow is then discarded from the window stack. If no
               saved window is available under the given index number,
               an error will occur. The *DeltaX* and *DeltaY* parameters
               give the *X* and *Y* offsets used to position the window on
               the screen. A value of 0 for both *DeltaX* and *DeltaY* posi-
               tions the window in the same place it was when it was
               saved with *StoreWindow*. A value of 1 for both *DeltaX*
               and *DeltaY* moves the window horizontally by 8 pixels
               and vertically by 1 pixel.

Restrictions   The value of *I* must lie between 1 and the constant
               MaxWindowsGlb (defined in TYPEDEF.SYS file).

See Also   ClearWindowStack
               LoadWindow
               StoreWindow

Example   RestoreWindow(4,10,0);
               restores the saved copy of window 4 to the active
               screen, at its previous *Y* position but 10 *X* window
               definition coordinates (80 pixels) to the right of its previ-
               ous *X* position.

RotatePolygon [MODPOLY.HGH]

Declaration **procedure** RotatePolygon(A:PlotArray; N:integer;
Angle:real);

Usage RotatePolygon(A,N,Angle);

Parameters *A* : polygon array to be rotated
N : number of polygon vertices
Angle : rotation angle in degrees

Function *RotatePolygon* rotates a polygon *A*, containing *N* vertices, around its center of gravity in a counterclockwise direction by *Angle* degrees. The center of gravity is calculated with the assumption that each vertex has equal weight.

Remarks When displaying a rotated polygon using *DrawPolygon*, the number of vertices should be given as a negative value; this guarantees that the polygon will be clipped at window boundaries.

Use *RotatePolygonAbout* to rotate a polygon about an arbitrary point.

Restrictions None

See Also DrawPolygon
RotatePolygonAbout
ScalePolygon
TranslatePolygon

Example RotatePolygon(Image,45,37.5);
changes the values of the 45 coordinate pairs in *Image* so that the polygon is rotated 37.5 degrees clockwise about its center of gravity.

RotatePolygonAbout [MODPOLY.HGH]

Declaration

procedure RotatePolygonAbout(A:PlotArray; N:integer;
Angle,X,Y:real);

Usage

RotatePolygonAbout(A,N,Angle,X,Y);

Parameters

A : polygon array to be rotated
N : number of polygon vertices
Angle : rotation angle in degrees
X,Y : world coordinates of point around which
polygon is rotated

Function

RotatePolygonAbout rotates a polygon *A* containing *N* vertices about an arbitrary point [*X,Y*], in a counterclockwise direction by *Angle* degrees.

Remarks

When displaying a rotated polygon with *DrawPolygon*, the number of vertices should be given as a negative value, to ensure clipping at window boundaries.

Restrictions

None

See Also

DrawPolygon
RotatePolygon
ScalePolygon
TranslatePolygon

Example

RotatePolygonAbout(Image,45,37.5,30.5,99);
changes the values of the 45 coordinate pairs in *Image* so that the polygon is rotated 37.5 degrees clockwise about world coordinages [30.5,99].

SaveScreen [GRAPHIX.SYS]

Declaration	**procedure** SaveScreen(FileName:WrkString);
Usage	SaveScreen(FileName);
Parameters	*FileName*: file name of screen (as saved on disk)
Function	*SaveScreen* stores a displayed or RAM screen on a floppy or hard disk. If a file with name *FileName* already exists, it is overwritten.
Restrictions	Screens saved with one version of the Turbo Graphix Toolbox are not necessarily compatible with any other version.
See Also	LoadScreen LoadWindow SaveWindow
Example	SaveScreen('PRETTY.PIC'); saves the active screen in a file called *PRETTY.PIC*.

SaveWindow [WINDOWS.SYS]

Declaration   **procedure** SaveWindow(I:integer; FileName:WrkString);

Usage   SaveWindow(I,FileName);

Parameters   *I*   : index of window to be saved
FileName : file name of window

Function   *SaveWindow* creates a file named by *FileName*, and saves window *I* in it. *FileName* can include an extension and a disk drive declaration (e.g., *a:FileName.xxx*) If a file named *FileName* already exists, it is overwritten. The size and position of the window are saved in the file, and are used when the window is loaded with *LoadWindow*, though the position can be changed if positive values are given for the *X* and *Y* coordinates when *LoadWindow* is called.

Remarks   Windows saved with different versions of the Turbo Graphix Toolbox will be compatible.

Restrictions   None

See Also   LoadScreen
LoadWindow
SaveScreen

Example   SaveWindow(15,'MENU.WIN');
saves window 15 in a file called *MENU.WIN*.

SaveWindowStack [WINDOWS.SYS]

Declaration   **procedure** SaveWindowStack(FileName:WrkString);

Usage   SaveWindowStack(FileName);

Parameters   *FileName* : file name of window stack

Function   *SaveWindowStack* stores a window stack on a floppy or hard disk. The contents of the stack include all defined and stored windows. The procedure automatically creates two files with extensions, *FileName.STK* (window stack) and *FileName.PTR* (pointer file). For this reason, you should not specify an extension for *FileName*, although a disk drive declaration can be specified. If a file with name *FileName* exists, it is overwritten.

Restrictions   Window stacks saved by different versions of the Turbo Graphix Toolbox will not necessarily be compatible.

See Also   LoadWindow
LoadWindowStack
SaveWindow

Example   SaveWindowStack ('WSTACK');
saves any windows that are currently stored in the window stack in two disk files, *WSTACK.STK* and *WSTACK.PTR.*

ScalePolygon [MODPOLY.HGH]

Declaration **procedure** ScalePolygon(Var A:PlotArray; N:integer;
XFactor,YFactor:real);

Usage ScalePolygon(A,N,XFactor,YFactor);

Parameters *A* : polygon array
N : number of polygon vertices
XFactor : multiplication factor (scaling) in *X* direction
YFactor : multiplication factor (scaling) in *Y* direction

Function *ScalePolygon* scales the lines that make up a polygon *A* by a proportional amount (*XFactor* and *YFactor*) in both horizontal (*X*) and vertical (*Y*) directions. The *X* coordinate of each of the *N* vertices is multiplied by *XFactor*, and the *Y* coordinate by *YFactor*.

Remarks When drawing a scaled polygon using *DrawPolygon*, the number of vertices should be given as a negative value, to ensure clipping at window boundaries.

Restrictions None

See Also DrawPolygon
RotatePolygon
RotatePolygonAbout
TranslatePolygon

Example ScalePolygon(Image,35,2,0.5);
changes the values of the 35 coordinate pairs in *Image* so that the polygon is stretched to twice its former width, and compressed to half its former height.

SelectScreen [KERNEL.SYS]

Declaration	**procedure** SelectScreen(I:integer);
Usage	SelectScreen(I);
Parameters	*I*: displayed or RAM screen
Function	*SelectScreen* selects either the displayed or RAM screen for drawing. If *I* is 1, the displayed screen is selected. If *I* is 2, the RAM screen is selected.
Remarks	The constant *RamScreenGlb*, defined in TYPEDEF.SYS, must be set to TRUE (the default) to enable a RAM screen.
Restrictions	Drawing is not visible on the RAM screen unless it is first copied to the displayed screen with *CopyScreen* or *SwapScreen*.
See Also	CopyScreen GetScreen SwapScreen
Example	SelectScreen(1); selects the displayed screen for subsequent drawing.

SelectWindow [KERNEL.SYS]

Declaration   **procedure** SelectWindow(I:integer);

Usage   SelectWindow(I);

Parameters   *I*: index of selected window ([1..*MaxWindowsGlb*])

Function   *SelectWindow* selects a window *I* for drawing. All subsequent drawing and window commands will refer to the selected window.

Remarks   If clipping is enabled with the *SetClippingOn* procedure, drawing is limited to the area inside the window.

Restrictions   The value of *I* must lie between 1 and the constant *MaxWindowsGlb* (defined in TYPEDEF.SYS FILE).

If a world is to be associated with a window, *SelectWorld* must be called before *SelectWindow*.

See Also   DefineWindow
SelectWorld

Example   SelectWindow(5);
selects window 5 for subsequent operations.

SelectWorld [KERNEL.SYS]

Declaration	**procedure** SelectWorld(I:integer);
Usage	SelectWorld(I);
Parameters	*I* : index of selected world ([1..*MaxWorldsGlb*])
Function	*SelectWorld* selects a world coordinate system, *I*, for the drawing commands that follow. This procedure must be followed by *SelectWindow* to associate the world with a window.
Restrictions	The value of *I* must lie between 1 and the constant *MaxWorldsGlb* (defined in TYPEDEF.SYS file).
See Also	DefineWindow DefineWorld FindWorld SelectWindow
Example	SelectWorld(3); SelectWindow(4); selects window 4, with world coordinate system 3, for subsequent operations.

SetAspect [KERNEL.SYS]

Declaration   **procedure** SetAspect(Aspect:real);

Usage   SetAspect(Aspect);

Parameters   *Aspect*: aspect ratio for circle

Function   *SetAspect* sets the value of the aspect ratio for drawing circles and ellipses. The default value for *Aspect* is the constant *AspectFactor*, defined in the GRAPHIX.SYS file. *SetAspect*(1) draws a true circle on any screen.

Remarks   The aspect ratio determines the shape of circles and ellipses. Changing the aspect ratio changes how tall a circle is. A machine-dependent constant, *AspectFactor*, specifies a ratio that should give a true circle for a particular physical screen. Drawing the same circle with aspect ratios of *AspectFactor* ÷ 2, *AspectFactor*, and *AspectFactor* × 2 will give three figures of the same width, but each twice as tall as the previous figure.

Restrictions   None

See Also   AspectFactor (constant)
DrawCartPie
DrawCircleSegment
DrawPolarPie
GetAspect
GetScreenAspect
SetScreenAspect

Example   SetAspect(1);
causes circles to be correctly proportioned on any screen.

SetBackground [GRAPHIX.SYS]

Declaration	**procedure** SetBackground(Pattern:byte);
Usage	SetBackground(Pattern);
Parameters	*Pattern*: bit pattern used for background (0 to 255)
Function	*SetBackground* determines the background pattern of the active window. There are 256 possible patterns, represented by the value of *Pattern*. Shading patterns consist of an 8-bit word repeated across each horizontal line to fill the window. The lowest (1) bit of the pattern is the rightmost pixel on the screen, and the highest (128) is the leftmost.
Remarks	A *Pattern* value of 0 creates a completely black background (which erases the contents of the window), while a value of 255 creates a white background.
Restrictions	None
See Also	DrawSquare
Example	SetBackground(17);

fills the active window with the pattern represented by the number 17: 00010001 binary (that is, 1 out of every 4 points are drawn).

SetBackground8 [GRAPHIX.SYS]

Declaration   **procedure** SetBackground8(Pattern:BackgroundArray);

Usage   SetBackground8(Pattern);

Parameters   *Pattern*: 8-byte background pattern

Function   *SetBackground* fills the active window with the specified bit pattern, *Pattern*. The *BackgroundArray* is an array of 8 bytes. The lowest 3 bits of the screen line number are used to determine which byte of the array to use; i.e.,the 0 array element is used on screen lines whose *Y* coordinates divide evenly by 8: for a screen line, *Yi*, array [*Yi* mod 8]. The lowest (1) bit of each byte of pattern is the rightmost, and the highest (128) is the leftmost pixel on the screen.

Restrictions   None

See Also   SetBackground

Example   **For** I:=0 **To** 7 **Do** BackgroundPattern [I]:=I*I;
            SetBackground8(BackgroundPattern);

This program fills the active window with the pattern below:

```
        +---------+
    0 |         |
    1 |        *|
    4 |     *   |
    9 |     *  *|
   16 |   *     |
   25 |   ** *|
   36 |   *  *  |
   49 |   ** *|
        +---------+
```

SetBackgroundColor [GRAPHIX.SYS]

Declaration	**procedure** SetBackgroundColor(Color:integer);
Usage	SetBackgroundColor(Color);
Parameters	*Color* : background color
Function	*SetBackgroundColor* chooses the background color ("black") from the colors available to your particular graphics card. Its value lies between the constants *MinBackground* and *MaxBackground* (defined in the GRAPHIX.SYS file).
Remarks	*InitGraphic* and *EnterGraphic* always reset colors to true black and white.
Restrictions	For IBM versions, the value of *SetBackgroundColor* must be 0 (true black) for the IBM color graphics adapter and the 3270 PC, or can be between 1 and 15 for the PCjr or Enhanced Graphics Adapter; the value of *SetForegroundColor* can be between 1 and 15. For Hercules, *SetBackgroundColor* and *SetForegroundColor* must both be 0, always black and white (or green or amber depending on the monitor). For Zenith, *SetBackgroundColor* must be 0 (true black), while *SetForegroundColor* can range between 1 and 7. Changing the colors changes the current display, and may have other system-dependent consequences; see Appendix A for more information.
See Also	Appendix A SetForegroundColor
Example	SetBackgroundColor (4); sets the color "black" to whatever color 4 represents for the particular graphics card installed. Any "black" images currently displayed immediately change to color 4.

SetBreakOff [KERNEL.SYS]

Declaration   **procedure** SetBreakOff;

Usage   SetBreakOff;

Function   *SetBreakOff* turns break mode off. When break mode is enabled with the *SetBreakOn* procedure, system errors cause the program to halt. With break mode off, the program proceeds, and it is up to the programmer to check for errors.

Remarks   The default state is break mode on.

                       GetErrorCode returns the code of the last error, or − 1 if no error has occurred since the last call to *GetErrorCode*. If a second error happens before the first is cleared, the first error code is lost. See *Error* for discussion.

Restrictions   None

See Also   Error
                       GetErrorCode
                       SetBreakOn
                       SetMessageOff
                       SetMessageOn

Example   SetBreakOff;
                       causes the program to continue in the event of a graphics error.

SetBreakOn [KERNEL.SYS]

Declaration	**procedure** SetBreakOn;
Usage	SetBreakOn;
Function	*SetBreakOn* turns break mode on. When an error occurs, the program halts and the error routine takes control of the program. The program counter value where the error occurred and an error code are displayed if *SetMessageOn* is enabled.
Remarks	The default state is break mode on. To allow a program to continue when an error occurs, *SetBreakOff* must be called.
Restrictions	None
See Also	Error GetErrorCode SetBreakOff SetMessageOff SetMessageOn
Example	SetBreakOn; causes graphics errors to abort the program.

SetClippingOff [KERNEL.SYS]

Declaration | **procedure** SetClippingOff;

Usage | SetClippingOff;

Function | *SetClippingModeOff* turns clipping mode off. All images are drawn in their entirety, regardless of window boundaries.

Remarks | The default state is clipping mode on.

SetClippingOff causes drawing to take place somewhat faster; however, this procedure should be used with caution, since an attempt to draw outside window boundaries using invalid coordinates can cause a system crash and/or overwriting of program memory.

Restrictions | None

See Also | Clip
Clipping
SetClippingOn
SetWindowModeOff
SetWindowModeOn

Example | SetClippingOff;
allows drawings to spill over the boundaries of the active window.

SetClippingOn [KERNEL.SYS]

Declaration	**procedure** SetClippingOn;
Usage	SetClippingOn;
Function	*SetClippingOn* turns clipping mode on. If part of a drawing falls outside the boundaries of the active window, it is not drawn.
Remarks	The default state is clipping mode on.
	Drawing takes place somewhat slower in this mode than with *SetClippingOff*, but it is the safer procedure to use, since drawings are prevented from encroaching on program or data memory.
Restrictions	None
See Also	Clip Clipping SetClippingOff SetWindowModeOff SetWindowModeOn
Example	SetClippingOn; causes any part of a drawing that strays outside window boundaries to be clipped.

SetColorBlack [KERNEL.SYS]

Declaration   **procedure** SetColorBlack;

Usage   SetColorBlack;

Function   *SetColorBlack* selects "black" as the current drawing color. All further text and graphics will be drawn in "black" until a call to *SetColorWhite*.

Remarks   Default drawing color is white.

"Black" can be any background color supported by your graphics card, except true white; see *SetForeground-Color*.

You may want to use the *SetBackground* procedure to fill a window with a non-black pattern before drawing in "black".

When *SetColorBlack* has been called, the *PointDrawn* function will return TRUE if the specified point is drawn in black.

Restrictions   For systems with color graphics cards, the color substituted for "black" cannot be true white.

See Also   DrawPoint
GetColor
PointDrawn
SetBackground
SetBackgroundColor
SetColorWhite
SetForegroundColor

Example   SetColorBlack;
causes subsequent images to be drawn in "black" (the background color).

SetColorWhite [KERNEL.SYS]

Declaration   **procedure** SetColorWhite;

Usage   SetColorWhite;

Function   *SetColorWhite* selects "white" as the current drawing color. All further text and graphics will be drawn in "white" until a call to *SetColorBlack*.

Remarks   Default drawing color is white.

"White" can be any foreground color supported by your graphics card, except true black; see *SetForegroundColor*.

You may want to use *SetBackground* to fill a window with a non-white pattern before drawing in white.

When *SetColorWhite* has been called, the *PointDrawn* function returns TRUE when the specified point is drawn in white.

Restrictions   On systems with color graphics cards, the color represented by "white" cannot be true black.

See Also   DrawPoint
GetColor
PointDrawn
SetBackground
SetBackgroundColor
SetColorBlack
SetForegroundColor

Example   SetColorWhite;
    causes subsequent images to be drawn in "white" (the foreground color).

SetForegroundColor [KERNEL.SYS]

Declaration
: **procedure** SetForegroundColor(Color:integer);

Usage
: SetForegroundColor(Color);

Parameters
: *Color*: color of displayed text and graphics

Function
: *SetForegroundColor* selects the drawing color from the colors available to your particular graphics card. Its value lies between the constants *MinForeground* and *MaxForeground* (defined in GRAPHIX.SYS).

Remarks
: *InitGraphic* and *EnterGraphic* always reset colors to true black and white.

  See the discussion under *SetBackgroundColor* for more information.

Restrictions
: See *SetBackgroundColor*.

See Also
: SetBackgroundColor
  SetColorBlack
  SetColorWhite

Example
: SetForegroundColor(9);
  sets the color "white" as whatever color 9 represents on the particular graphics card installed. Any "white" images currently displayed immediately change to color 9.

SetHeaderOff [KERNEL.SYS]

Declaration   **procedure** SetHeaderOff;

Usage   SetHeaderOff;

Function   *SetHeaderOff* suppresses the display of window headers and footers until a call to *SetHeaderOn*. This means that *DrawBorder* will not display any header or footer unless *SetHeaderOn* has been called.

Remarks   The default state is header mode off.

Windows currently displayed on the screen are not affected by *SetHeaderOff*.

See *DefineHeader* for how to define headers.

Restrictions   None

See Also   DefineHeader
DrawBorder
RemoveHeader
SetHeaderOn
SetHeaderToBottom
SetHeaderToTop

Example   SetHeaderOff;
subsequent calls to *DrawBorder* will not draw a header for any window, even if a header is defined.

SetHeaderOn [KERNEL.SYS]

Declaration	**procedure** SetHeaderOn;
Usage	SetHeaderOn;
Function	*SetHeaderOn* allows window headers and footers to be displayed when *DrawBorder* is called.
Remarks	Default state is header mode off.
	SetHeaderOn does not affect windows currently displayed on the screen.
	See *DefineHeader* for how to define window headers.
Restrictions	None
See Also	DefineHeader DrawBorder RemoveHeader SetHeaderOff SetHeaderToBottom SetHeaderToTop
Example	SetHeaderOn; subsequent calls to *DrawBorder* will draw a header for any window for which a header is defined.

SetHeaderToBottom [KERNEL.SYS]

Declaration **procedure** SetHeaderToBottom;

Usage SetHeaderToBottom;

Function *SetHeaderToBottom* displays all headers at the bottom edge of windows, i.e., as footers, when *DrawBorder* is called.

Remarks Headers are displayed at the top of windows by default.

This procedure does not affect windows currently displayed on the screen.

See *DefineHeader* for how to define window headers.

Restrictions None

See Also DefineHeader
DrawBorder
RemoveHeader
SetHeaderOff
SetHeaderOn
SetHeaderToTop

Example SetHeaderToBottom;
subsequent calls to *DrawBorder* will draw window headers at the bottom of windows.

SetHeaderToTop [KERNEL.SYS]

Declaration   **procedure** SetHeaderToTop;

Usage   SetHeaderToTop;

Function   *SetHeaderToTop* allows window headers to be drawn at the top edge of windows when *DrawBorder* is called.

Remarks   Headers are displayed at the top of windows by default.

      SetHeaderToTop does not affect windows currently displayed on the screen.

      See *DefineHeader* for how to define window headers.

Restrictions   None

See Also   DefineHeader
DrawBorder
RemoveHeader
SetHeaderOff
SetHeaderOn
SetHeaderToBottom

Example   SetHeaderToTop;
      subsequent calls to *DrawBorder* will draw window headers at the top of windows.

SetLineStyle [KERNEL.SYS]

Declaration **procedure** SetLineStyle(LS:integer);

Usage SetLineStyle(LS);

Parameters *LS*: one of five possible line styles

Function *SetLineStyle* selects one of five available line styles for drawing lines; custom patterns can also be designed. Patterns consist of eight repeating pixels. The five predefined patterns are:

```
0: **************** (unbroken line)
1: *   *   *   *   (dotted line)
2: *****    *****   (dashed line)
3: ***  *  ***  *  (dash-dot-dash-dot)
4: *** *** *** *** (short dashes)
```

Any integer value larger than 4 is interpreted according to the modulo function; that is, the high-order byte of the integer is discarded, and the remaining 8 bits specify the pattern to be repeated. The lowest bit comes first. Thus, a linestyle of 100 decimal is 01100100 binary, for a linestyle of

```
**  *   **  *   **  *   **  *   **  *  . . .
```

Remarks *GetLineStyle* returns the linestyle as a value of 0 to 4 for the predefined patterns, and 256 + pattern for custom patterns.

Restrictions None

See Also GetLineStyle

Example SetLineStyle(1);
    sets the line style to pattern 1, a dotted line.

SetLineStyle(117);
    sets the line style to the bit pattern represented by decimal 117, binary 01110101, as follows:

```
*** * * *** * *   . . .
```

SetMessageOff [KERNEL.SYS]

Declaration	**procedure** SetMessageOff;
Usage	SetMessageOff;
Function	*SetMessageOff* suppresses the display of complete error messages. However, if break mode is enabled with the *SetBreakOn* procedure, a brief, non-explanatory message is displayed. The following table shows how error messages are handled by *SetMessageOff* and *SetMessageOn*, in conjunction with *SetBreakOn* and *SetBreakOff*.

	SetMessageOn	SetMessageOff
SetBreakOn Enabled	Complete error message including traceback displayed; halts.	"Graphics error ", proc, code displayed; program halts.
SetBreakOff Enabled	Complete error message displayed on line 24; program continues with no traceback.	No message; program continues.

Remarks	The default state is message mode on.
	The reason a brief message is displayed with *SetMessageOff* is so that, if you sell a program written with the Turbo Graphix Toolbox, your end users can provide you with information about the cause of an error.
Restrictions	None
See Also	Error GetErrorCode SetBreakOff SetBreakOn
Example	SetMessageOff; if break mode is off, errors will not cause error messages to be displayed. If break mode is on, only a brief error message is displayed before the program is aborted.

SetMessageOn [KERNEL.SYS]

Declaration	**procedure** SetMessageOn;
Usage	SetMessageOn;
Function	*SetMessageOn* allows complete error messages to be displayed, whether break mode is enabled or not. See the table under *SetMessageOff* for an explanation of how error messages are handled by the *SetMessage* procedures.
Remarks	Default state is message mode on.
Restrictions	None
See Also	Error GetErrorCode SetBreakOff SetBreakOn SetMessageOff
Example	SetMessageOn; If break mode is off, errors will cause error messages to be displayed on screen line 24. If break mode is on, error messages will include the name of the procedure and the nature of the error, along with a a traceback.

SetScreenAspect [KERNEL.SYS]

Declaration	**procedure** SetScreenAspect(Aspect:real);
Usage	SetScreenAspect(Aspect);
Parameters	*Aspect*: aspect ratio for circle, in pixels
Function	*SetScreenAspect* sets the value of the aspect ratio, in pixels, for drawing circles and ellipses. *SetScreenAspect*(1) makes a circle or ellipse that is equal in pixel width and height.
Remarks	This procedure is used for applications in which you need to create a circle or ellipse that is proportional in terms of pixels. Note that such a circle is not necessarily correctly proportioned when viewed on the screen; a certain number of consecutive pixels displayed horizontally is quite a bit shorter in length than the same number vertically. An aspect ratio of about 0.6 often gives a truer circle on the screen. Use *SetAspect* to draw visually proportioned circles on a particular screen.
Restrictions	None
See Also	AspectFactor (constant) DrawCartPie DrawCircleSegment DrawPolarPie GetAspect GetScreenAspect SetAspect
Example	SetScreenAspect(1); causes circles to have the same number of vertical as horizontal pixels.

SetVStep [KERNEL.SYS]

Declaration	**procedure** SetVStep(Step:integer);
Usage	SetVStep(Step);
Parameters	*Step* : number of vertical pixels moved by a window at one time
Function	*SetVStep* specifies the vertical distance, in pixels, that a window moves at one time. *Step* can be any integer value larger than 0. Small *Step* values cause smooth, slower window movement, while larger values cause faster, but somewhat jerkier movement.
Remarks	The default value for *VStep* depends on the resolution produced by the particular graphics card installed in your system. This default value is set by the constant *IVStep* in GRAPHIX.SYS. See Appendix A for more information on hardware configurations.
	If a window is moved a distance that is not a multiple of the current *VStep* value, it is moved by multiples of *VStep* towards its destination, then one final, variable-length *Step* to reach its destination. See *MoveVer*.
Restrictions	The value for *Step* must be a positive integer.
See Also	Appendix A MoveVer
Example	SetVStep(12); causes vertical window movement (with the *MoveVer* procedure) to take place in 12-pixel increments.

SetWindowModeOff [KERNEL.SYS]

Declaration   **procedure** SetWindowModeOff;

Usage   SetWindowModeOff;

Function   *SetWindowModeOff* allows drawing to take place on the screen, in absolute screen coordinates, rather than in a window. Drawings are not clipped at window boundaries unless clipping is enabled with the *SetClippingOn* procedure.

Remarks   Default state is window mode on.

                Since no clipping is performed when *SetWindowModeOff* has been called, drawing takes place somewhat faster. However, this procedure should be used with caution, since invalid coordinates can cause drawing to encroach on program memory or crash the system.

Restrictions   None

See Also   DefineWindow
                SelectWindow
                SetClippingOff
                SetClippingOn
                SetWindowModeOn

Example   SetWindowModeOff;
                turns window mode off, so that subsequent coordinates are calculated as screen coordinates, with no clipping at window boundaries.

SetWindowModeOn [KERNEL.SYS]

Declaration   **procedure** SetWindowModeOn;

Usage   SetWindowModeOn;

Function   *SetWindowModeOn* allows you to draw in a window, in world coordinates. Drawings are clipped at the active window boundaries if clipping is enabled with the *SetClippingOn* procedure.

Remarks   Default state is window mode on.

                Although drawing takes place somewhat slower with window mode on, *SetWindowModeOn* is the safer procedure to use, since clipping at window boundaries is possible and program memory therefore protected.

Restrictions   None

See Also   DefineWindow
                SelectWindow
                SetClippingOff
                SetClippingOn
                SetWindowModeOff

Example   SetWindowModeOn;
                turns window mode on, so that world coordinate systems can be used, and drawings can be clipped at window boundaries.

Spline [SPLINE.HGH]

Declaration	**procedure** Spline(A:PlotArray; N:integer; X1,XM:real; var B:PlotArray; M:integer);

Usage   Spline(A,N,X1,XM,B,M);

Parameters

A   : polygon array (base points)
N   : number of base points
X1 : index value from which interpolation begins
XM : index of value where interpolation ends
B   : resultant spline polygon array (to be filled with calculated spline)
M   : number of points to calculate in spline array

Function

When polygons are plotted with a few data points, the connection of these points sometimes results in a vague, angular representation of the true curve. One way to resolve this problem is to evaluate additional base points to smooth the graph plot. However, the calculation time involved in this method may be prohibitive.

The spline functions use smoothing polynomials to generate additional base points. Spline functions are stable in all parts of the definition interval and, unlike many other polynomials, they do not tend to have strong oscillations.

The *Spline* procedure calculates smoothed curves from corresponding data. The number and density of the interpolated points created by the spline function is arbitrary.

To use the *Spline* procedure, first pass a *PlotArray* and the number of points in the array (*N*). *X1* and *XM* specify the starting and ending points, respectively, for the interpolation. The *PlotArray B* receives the resultant interpolated curve. The calculated base points are evenly spaced between the starting and ending points of the input curve.

The spline function is calculated with the following formula:

$$p_n(x) = y_1 \frac{(x-x_2) \cdots (x-x_n)}{(x_1-x_2) \cdots (x_1-x_n)} + y_2 \frac{(x-x_1)(x-x_3) \cdots (x-x_n)}{(x_2-x_1)(x_2-x_3) \cdots (x_2-x_n)}$$
$$+ \cdots + y_n \frac{(x-x_1) \cdots (x-x_{n-1})}{(x_n-x_1) \cdots (x_n-x_{n-1})}$$

Restrictions   For the base points of the interpolation the following con-
                 ditions apply:

$$X1 \geq X2 \qquad XN - 1 \leq XM$$

$X2/N - 1$ represents the second/second to the last
point of the polygon. The interpolation may only be car-
ried out within that interval.

Example   Spline(RoughCurve,10,5.7,213,SmootherCurve,50);
                 interpolates a smoothed 50-point curve from the given
                 10-point curve, over the *X* range of 5.7 to 213.

StoreWindow [WINDOWS.SYS]

Declaration   **procedure** StoreWindow(Window:integer);

Usage   StoreWindow(Window);

Parameters   *Window*: index of window to be saved
[1..*MaxWindowsGlb*]

Function   *StoreWindow* saves a given window in the window stack. The procedure checks the window memory to see if sufficient space is available to store the window. If space is not available, an error occurs and the window is not stored. If a previously stored window and the active window share the same index number, the active window overwrites the stored window.

Remarks   Storing a window does not affect the screen display.

Stored windows are dynamically allocated on the heap with Turbo Pascal's *GetMem* and *FreeMem* procedures. Windows are always allocated in multiples of 1K (1024) bytes. Because the *StoreWindow* and *RestoreWindow* procedures use *GetMem* and *FreeMem*, your program must not use the Mark/Release method of memory management.

Turbo Pascal's built-in function, *MaxAvail* can be used to determine whether a window will fit on the stack. *MaxAvail* returns the size of the largest chunk of free memory on the stack, expressed in paragraphs (16-byte chunks). By comparing *MaxAvail* to *WindowSize*, which returns the amount of memory required by a particular window, you can tell if there is sufficient room on the stack for the window. That is,

If 16.0*MaxAvail > WindowSize(i) **then** ok

Restrictions   The value for *Window* must lie between 1 and the constant *MaxWindowsGlb* (defined in the TYPEDEF.SYS file). If an illegal window number is given for Window, or if the stack is out of space, an error occurs.

See Also   RestoreWindow
            WindowSize
            WindowStackSize

Example   StoreWindow(12);
            causes window 12 to be copied to the window stack
            for later retrieval.

SwapScreen [GRAPHIX.SYS]

Declaration	**procedure** SwapScreen;
Usage	SwapScreen;
Function	*SwapScreen* exchanges the contents of the displayed screen with the contents of the RAM screen.
Remarks	The active screen is not changed by *SwapScreen*. This means that, if you are drawing on one screen and call *SwapScreen* while you are still drawing, the part of the drawing that is complete is moved to the inactive screen, but subsequent drawing takes place on the active screen.
Restrictions	This procedure can only be used if a RAM screen is allocated, i.e., *RamScreenGlb* is TRUE (defined in TYPEDEF.SYS file).
See Also	CopyScreen LoadScreen SaveScreen SelectScreen
Example	SwapScreen; swaps the contents of the displayed and RAM screens.

TextDown [GRAPHIX.SYS]

Declaration	**function** TextDown(TY, Boundary:integer):integer;
Usage	TextDown(TY,Boundary);
Parameters	*TY* : *Y* coordinate of given machine-dependent text that is to be within a window *Boundary* : desired number of pixels between text and bottom edge of window
Function	*TextDown* uses the given *Y* text coordinate, *TY*, and the number of pixels, *Boundary*, that you want to have between the text and the bottom edge of the window, to calculate a *Y* window definition coordinate. The function then returns the *Y* coordinate of the bottom edge of a window that is at least *Boundary* pixels below the bottom edge of text coordinate *TY*.
Remarks	Along with *TextLeft*, *TextRight*, and *TextUp*, this function is used to fit and align text within a window. It is particularly useful with the Hercules version of the Turbo Graphix Toolbox, since Hercules text is defined on 9-pixel boundaries, while windows are defined on 8-pixel boundaries; this 1-pixel offset can cause alignment problems. If you want a uniform space between your text and all four window boundaries, use the *DefineTextWindow* procedure. See Appendix A for more information.
Restrictions	None
See Also	Appendix A DefineTextWindow TextLeft TextRight TextUp
Example	I:=TextDown(16,2); sets *I* to the *Y* screen coordinate at the bottom of row 16, with a boundary of 2 pixels between the text and the window.

TextLeft [GRAPHIX.SYS]

Declaration	**function** TextLeft(TX, Boundary:integer):integer;
Usage	TextLeft(TX,Boundary);
Parameters	*TX* : *X* coordinate of given machine-dependent text that is to be inside a window *Boundary* : desired number of pixels between text and left edge of window

Function

TextLeft uses the given *X* text coordinate, *TX*, and the number of pixels, *Boundary*, that you want to have between the text and the left edge of the window, to calculate an *X* window definition coordinate. The function then returns the *X* coordinate of the left edge of a window that is at least *Boundary* pixels to the left of the left edge of text coordinate *TX*.

Remarks

Along with *TextDown, TextRight,* and *TextUp*, this function is used to fit and align text within a window. It is particularly useful with the Hercules version of the Turbo Graphix Toolbox, since Hercules text is defined on 9-pixel boundaries, while windows are defined on 8-pixel boundaries; this 1-pixel offset can create alignment problems. If you want a uniform space between your text and all four window boundaries, use the *DefineTextWindow* procedure. See Appendix A for more information.

Restrictions

None

See Also

Appendix A
DefineTextWindow
TextDown
TextRight
TextUp

Example

I:=TextLeft(LeftMargin,0);
    sets *I* to the *X* screen coordinate that corresponds to the left edge of column *LeftMargin*.

TextRight [GRAPHIX.SYS]

Declaration	**function** TextRight(TX,Boundary:integer):integer;
Usage	TextRight(TX,Boundary);

Parameters
: *TX* : *X* coordinate of given machine-dependent text that is to be inside a window
Boundary : desired number of pixels between text and right edge of window

Function
: *TextRight* uses the given *X* text coordinate, *TX*, and the number of pixels, *Boundary*, that you want to have between the text and the right edge of the window, to calculate an *X* window definition coordinate. The function then returns the *X* coordinate of the right edge of a window that is at least *Boundary* pixels to the right of the right edge of text coordinate *TX*.

Remarks
: Along with *TextDown, TextLeft* and *TextUp*, this function is used to fit and align text within a window. It is particularly useful with the Hercules version of the Turbo Graphix Toolbox, since Hercules text is defined on 9-pixel boundaries, while windows are defined on 8-pixel boundaries; this 1-pixel offset can create alignment problems. If you want a uniform space between your text and all four window boundaries, use the *DefineTextWindow* procedure. See Appendix A for more information.

Restrictions
: None

See Also
: Appendix A
DefineTextWindow
TextDown
TextLeft
TextUp

Example
: TextRight(68,1);
sets *J* to the *X* screen coordinate that is at least 1 pixel to the right of column 68.

TextUp [GRAPHIX.SYS]

Declaration **function** TextUp(TY, Boundary:integer):integer;

Usage TextUp(TY,Boundary);

Parameters *TY* : *Y* coordinate of given machine-dependent
text that is to be within a window
Boundary : desired number of pixels between text
and top edge of window

Function *TextUp* uses the given *Y* text coordinate, *TY*, and the number of pixels, *Boundary*, that you want to have between the text and the top edge of the window, to calculate a *Y* window definition coordinate. The function then returns the *Y* coordinate of the upper edge of a window that is at least *Boundary* pixels above the top edge of text coordinate *TY*.

Remarks Along with *TextLeft, TextRight,* and *TextDown,* this function is used to fit and align text within a window. It is particularly useful with the Hercules version of the Turbo Graphix Toolbox, since Hercules text is defined on 9-pixel boundaries, while windows are defined on 8-pixel boundaries; this 1-pixel offset can create alignment problems. If you want a uniform space between your text and all four window boundaries, use the *DefineTextWindow* procedure. See Appendix A for more information.

Restrictions None

See Also Appendix A
DefineTextWindow
TextDown
TextLeft
TextRight

Example U:=TextUp(TopLine,HeaderSize);
sets *U* to the *Y* screen coordinate that is *HeaderSize* pixels above row *TopLine.*

TranslatePolygon [MODPOLY.HGH]

Declaration	**procedure** TranslatePolygon(Var A:PlotArray; N:integer; DeltaX,DeltaY:real);
Usage	TranslatePolygon(A,N,DeltaX,DeltaY);
Parameters	*A* : polygon array *N* : number of polygon vertices *DeltaX* : displacement in *X* direction *DeltaY* : displacement in *Y* direction
Function	*TranslatePolygon* moves all polygon line endpoints by adding *X* and *Y* displacements, thus moving the entire polygon both vertically by *DeltaX* and horizontally by *DeltaY*.
Remarks	When drawing a translated polygon using *DrawPolygon*, the number of vertices should be passed as a negative value, so that *DrawPolygon* clips the polygon at window boundaries.
Restrictions	None
See Also	DrawPolygon RotatePolygon ScalePolygon
Example	TranslatePolygon(Image,73,25,-19.8) changes the values of the 73 coordinate pairs in *Image* so that the polygon is moved 25 *X* units to the right, and 19.8 *Y* units towards the top of the screen.

WindowMode [KERNEL.SYS]

Declaration	**function** WindowMode:boolean;
Usage	WindowMode;
Function	*WindowMode* returns the window status: TRUE if *WindowModeOn* has been called, FALSE if *WindowModeOff* has been called.
Restrictions	None
See Also	SetWindowModeOff SetWindowModeOn
Example	B:=WindowMode; *B* is TRUE if window mode is currently enabled.

WindowSize [WINDOWS.SYS]

Declaration	**function** WindowSize (Nr:integer):integer;
Usage	WindowSize(Nr);
Parameters	*Nr* : index of window [1..*MaxWindowsGlb*]
Function	*WindowSize* calculates the size of a window in bytes. In a window stack operation, this size is compared to the available window stack space to see if there is sufficient room for the window in the stack; if not, an error occurs.

The formula used for this calculation is:

$$WindowSize: = (Y2 - Y1 + 1)\ (X2 - X1)$$

The value returned is rounded up to the nearest 1,024 to match with the amount of space the window will consume if it is saved on the window stack. [*X1,Y1*] are the coordinates of the left upper corner of the window, and [*X2,Y2*] are the coordinates of the right lower corner of the window.

Restrictions	The value of *Nr* must lie between 1 and the constant *MaxWindowsGlb* (defined in the TYPEDEF.SYS file).
See Also	ClearWindowStack RestoreWindow StoreWindow WindowStackSize
Example	I:=WindowSize(3); *I* contains the number of bytes needed to store window 3 in the window stack.

WindowX [KERNEL.SYS]

Declaration	**function** WindowX(X:real):integer;
Usage	WindowX(X);
Parameters	*X* : *X* world coordinate
Function	*WindowX* translates an *X* world coordinate into an absolute screen coordinate and returns this value.
Restrictions	None
See Also	DefineWorld DefineWindow SelectWindow SelectWorld
Example	X:=WindowX(X1); converts the world coordinate *X1* to a screen coordinate and stores the value in *X*.

WindowY [KERNEL.SYS]

Declaration   **function** WindowY(Y:real):integer;

Usage   WindowY(Y);

Parameters   *Y* : *Y* world coordinate

Function   *WindowY* translates a *Y* coordinate from world coordi-
                nate to absolute screen coordinates, and returns this
                value.

Restrictions   None

Example   Y:=WindowY(Yl);
                converts world coordinate *Y1* to a screen coordinate
                and stores the value in *Y*.

Notes:

Turbo Graphix Toolbox Owner's Handbook

Appendix A.
HARDWARE CONFIGURATIONS
AND COMPATIBILITY PROBLEMS

This section describes three of the hardware configurations that support the Turbo Graphix Toolbox. Problems or considerations specific to the IBM, Hercules, and Zenith implementations are first discussed separately; a detailed discussion about compatibility between different hardware configurations follows.

Complete information about the constants, types, procedures and functions mentioned in this Appendix can be found in Chapter 3.

The IBM Color Graphics Card

The IBM Color Graphics card supports a hardware environment with the following general characteristics:

- Screen is 640 pixels wide by 200 pixels tall.

- Default step (increment) for vertical window movement (as defined in the constant *IVStep*) is 2 pixels.

- A RAM screen is enabled (constant *RamScreenGlb* = TRUE) and is placed in normal RAM.

Constants take the following default values with the IBM card:

AspectFactor	= 0.44	MinForeground	= 1
HardwareGrafBase	= $B800	RamScreenGlb	= TRUE
IVStep	= 2	ScreenSizeGlb	= 8191
MaxBackground	= *	XMaxGlb	= 79
MaxForeground	= 15	XScreenMaxGlb	= 639
MinBackground	= 0	YMaxGlb	= 199

* depends on version

Color

The different IBM versions of the Turbo Graphix Toolbox allow either one background color, true black (constants *MinBackground* and *MaxBackground* are both 0), or up to fifteen background colors (*MinBackground* = 0, *MaxBackground* = 15); fifteen foreground colors are available (*MinForeground* = 1, *MaxForeground* = 15), except with the PCjr, which allows only black or white for the foreground color. *MaxForeground* is the default value, set both by the *InitGraphic* and *EnterGraphic* procedures. The following table lists the colors for the IBM Color/Graphics Adapter (CGA), the PCjr, the Enhanced Graphics Adapter (EGA), and the 3270 PC.

Foreground Colors

	CGA	PCjr	EGA	3270 PC
0	Black	Black	Black	Black
1	Blue	White	Blue	Blue
2	Green	Black	Green	Green
3	Cyan	White	Cyan	Turquoise
4	Red	Black	Red	Red
5	Magenta	White	Magenta	Pink
6	Brown	Black	Brown	Yellow
7	Light gray	White	Light gray	White
8	Dark gray	Black	Dark gray	Black
9	Light blue	White	Light blue	Blue
10	Light green	Black	Light green	Green
11	Light cyan	White	Light cyan	Turquoise
12	Light red	Black	Light red	Red
13	Light magenta	White	Light magenta	Pink
14	Yellow	Black	Yellow	Yellow
15	White	White	White	White

Background Colors

	CGA	PCjr	EGA	3270 PC
0	Black	Black	Black	Black
1	Black	Blue	Blue	Black
2	Black	Green	Green	Black
3	Black	Cyan	Cyan	Black
4	Black	Red	Red	Black
5	Black	Magenta	Magenta	Black
6	Black	Brown	Brown	Black
7	Black	Light gray	Light gray	Black
8	Black	Dark gray	Dark gray	Black
9	Black	Light blue	Light blue	Black
10	Black	Light green	Light green	Black
11	Black	Light cyan	Light cyan	Black
12	Black	Light red	Light red	Black
13	Black	Light magenta	Light magenta	Black
14	Black	Yellow	Yellow	Black
15	Black	White	White	Black

Text

In addition to the standard 4x6-pixel font used by Turbo Graphix, the IBM card allows higher quality text characters to be drawn in the normal IBM Color/graphics adapter font. These characters take the form of 8x8-pixel cells, and can only be drawn at *X* and *Y* coordinates that are multiples of 8 pixels. Since windows are also defined on 8-pixel horizontal boundaries, the higher quality text can be aligned exactly with windows.

Text can be moved vertically to any screen position using the window movement procedure *MoveVer*. Unlike the 4x6-pixel font, IBM text is never clipped at window boundaries.

The Hercules Monochrome Graphics Card

The Hercules Monochrome Graphics card supports a hardware environment with the following general characteristics:

- Screen is 720 pixels wide by 350 pixels tall.

- Default step (increment) for vertical window movement is 5 pixels (as specified by the constant *IVStep*).

- A RAM screen is allocated (constant *RamScreenGlb* = TRUE). The RAM screen can be placed in normal RAM (default) or on the Hercules card itself, as determined by the initialized variable *RamScreenInCard* in the GRAPHIX.HGC file. If *RamScreenInCard* is TRUE, the RAM screen is on the Hercules card; if FALSE, it is in normal RAM. If you change *RamScreenInCard* to TRUE, your Hercules card must be placed in the "full" configuration.

Constants take the following values with the Hercules card:

AspectFactor	= 0.75	RamScreenGlb	= TRUE
HardwareGrafBase	= $B000	* RamScreenInCard	= FALSE
IVStep	= 5	ScreenSizeGlb	= 16383
MaxBackground	= 0	XMaxGlb	= 89
MaxForeground	= 1	XScreenMaxGlb	= 719
MinBackground	= 0	YMaxGlb	= 349
MinForeground	= 1		

* Specific to the Hercules implementation

Color

The Hercules card does not support color. Neither background nor foreground color can be changed; both *MinBackground* and *MaxBackground* are set to 0 (black) and both *MinForeground* and *MaxForeground* are set to 1 (white).

Text

In addition to the standard 4x6-pixel font used by Turbo Graphix to draw window headers and footers, the Hercules card allows higher quality text characters to be drawn on the screen in the normal Hercules font. These characters take the form of 9x14 pixel cells, can only be drawn at text coordinates that start at [0,0], and move in steps (increments) of 9 horizontal pixels by 14 vertical pixels. Using the window movement procedures *MoveHor* and *MoveVer*, you can move text to any desired screen location. However, because Hercules horizontal text coordinates are at multiples of 9 pixels, and window definition coordinates are at multiples of 8, care must be taken when attempting to draw text inside a window; the alignment of text with the window may be slightly skewed due to the repeating 1-pixel offset of text.

Unlike the 4x6-pixel Turbo Graphix font, Hercules text is never clipped at window boundaries.

Special Notes

Though the Hercules card normally has a resolution of 720x348, through special programming, the Hercules version of the Turbo Graphix Toolbox changes the resolution to 720x352; the last two vertical pixels are ignored by the program, thus giving a resolution of 720x350. There are a few monitors that may not be able to display this higher resolution. If your monitor loses its horizontal hold when you use Turbo Graphix, you must change two constants in GRAPHIX.SYS: *YMaxGlb* should be changed from 349 to 347, and *VRowsGlb* should be changed from $58 to $57. Be sure to change both constants.

With the Hercules card, if a program terminates while in graphics mode, part of the current graphic display will remain on the screen, and part will be erased. This is because MS-DOS does not understand that the computer is in graphics mode, and will try to use the Hercules card as if it were in text mode. To prevent this, you must use the DOS command MODE MONO or run the program HFIX.COM (on the Turbo Graphix Toolbox distribution disk).

Suppose your program terminates due to an I/O or runtime error. In this case, you will probably want to see the error message, so you should use HFIX.COM, which displays the error message, rather than MODE MONO, which clears the screen. However, part of the error message may scroll off the screen. One way to capture the error message before it disappears is to use the Shift-Printscreen sequence. DOS will then display the text screen even though there is also a graphics display.

The Zenith Color Graphics Card

The Zenith Color Graphics card supports a hardware environment with the following general characteristics:

- Screen is 640 pixels wide by 225 pixels tall.

- Default step (increment) for vertical window movement (as defined in the constant *IVStep*) is 3 pixels.

- A RAM screen is enabled (constant *RamScreenGlb* = TRUE) and is placed in normal RAM.

Constants take the following default values with the Zenith card:

AspectFactor	= .495	MinForeground	= 1
HardwareGrafBase	= $C000	RamScreenGlb	= TRUE
IVStep	= 3	ScreenSizeGlb	= 24575
MaxBackground	= 0	XMaxGlb	= 79
MaxForeground	= 7	XScreenMaxGlb	= 639
MinBackground	= 0	YMaxGlb	= 224

Color

The Zenith version of the Turbo Graphix Toolbox allows only one background color, true black (constants *MinBackground* and *MaxBackground* must both be 0); seven foreground colors are available (*MinForeground* = 1, *MaxForeground* = 7). *MaxForeground* is the default value, set both by the *InitGraphic* and *EnterGraphic* procedures. Available colors are:

1 Blue
2 Green
3 Cyan
4 Red
5 Magenta
6 Yellow
7 White

Text

In addition to the standard 4x6-pixel font used by Turbo Graphix, the Zenith card allows higher quality text characters to be drawn in the normal Zenith font. These characters take the form of 8x9-pixel cells, and can only be drawn at *X* and *Y* coordinates that are multiples of 8 horizontal by 9 vertical pixels. Since windows are also defined on horizontal 8-pixel boundaries, the higher quality text can be aligned exactly with windows.

Text can be moved vertically to any screen position using the window movement procedure *MoveVer*. Unlike the 4x6-pixel font, Zenith text is never clipped at window boundaries.

Compatibility Issues

This section discusses the problems involved with writing a program for more than one version of the Turbo Graphix Toolbox, and offers suggestions for resolving those problems.

Screen Size

Probably the biggest problem involved with writing programs for different Turbo Graphix versions is that the graphics cards support different screen sizes. This is especially troublesome for drawings that use absolute screen coordinates. You could define a window and display the drawing using world coordinates, which partially resolves the problem; however, the placement of the window itself depends on the resolution of the screen. For instance, on the IBM Color/graphics adapter, a window with its upper left corner at [20,50] and lower right corner at [60,150] is a centered window that is approximately 1/4 the size of the screen. On the Hercules card, the same window would be placed slightly further to the left on the screen, and significantly closer to the top, and would take up only about 1/8 of the screen.

One solution to this problem would be to use the global constants *XMaxGlb* and *YMaxGlb* to standardize the placement of the window. The statement

```
DefineWindow(1,XMaxGlb Div 4,YMaxGlb Div 4,XMaxGlb*3 Div 4,
  YMaxGlb*3 Div 4);
```

would define a centered window that takes up approximately 1/4 of the screen, regardless of the actual screen size.

Text Placement

Another potential compatibility problem is text placement. Although the 4x6-pixel text can be placed at any screen coordinates with the *DrawText* procedure, or at any world coordinates with the *DrawTextW* procedure, recreating the same text on different screens is difficult. This is because the size of the characters may also have to be adjusted. The machine-dependent font is correctly proportioned for the graphics card in use, though it can be difficult to place. For example, suppose, on the IBM Color adapter version, that a window is to be defined that will enclose text coordinates [10,2] through [20,4]. The following statement shows one way to define that window:

```
DefineWindow(1,(XMaxGlb*10) Div 80,(YMaxGlb*2) Div 25,
  (XMaxGlb*20) Div 80,(YMaxGlb*4) Div 25);
```

This statement is equivalent to

```
DefineWindow(1,(79*10) Div 80,(199*2) Div 25,(79*20) Div 80,
            (199*4) Div 25);
```

or

```
DefineWindow(1,(790) Div  80,(398) Div 25,(1580) Div  80,
            (796) Div 25);
```

or

```
DefineWindow(1,9,15,19,31);
```

The screen coordinates above are (72,15,159,31) (the *X* screen coordinate is greater by 7 because it includes the entire byte at that coordinate).

On the IBM version, text is drawn at every 8 pixels in both directions, so the screen coordinates to use for a window that includes text coordinates [10,2] through [20,4] are (80,16,167,39). If (XMaxGlb + 1) and (YMaxGlb + 1) were used in the first statement,

```
DefineWindow(1,((XMaxGlb+1)*10)   Div  80,((YMaxGlb+1)*2)  Div   25,
            ((XMaxGlb+1)*20) Div 80,((YMaxGlb+1)*4) Div 25);
```

the resulting window would be at screen coordinates (80,16,167,32), which would align the text more exactly with the window. Adding 7 to the final *Y* coordinate makes it exact:

```
DefineWindow(1,((XMaxGlb+1)*10)   Div  80,((YMaxGlb+1)*2)  Div   25,
            ((XMaxGlb+1)*20) Div 80,((YMaxGlb+1)*4) Div 25 + 7);
```

However, if the last statement is used on the Hercules card, the final coordinates come out as (88,28,183,63), which is close to the correct (90,28,188,64)—but not close enough. Text drawn in that window would spill over the right and bottom edges of the window. But the correct window (90,28,188,64) is an illegal window! The first *X* coordinate, 90, is not a multiple of 8, and the second, 188, is not 1 less than a multiple of 8.

Because of the complexity involved in choosing a window to fit text, four functions are provided that choose window definition coordinates based on text coordinates. Each function is given a text coordinate and a minimum boundary value. The function returns a window definition coordinate that will contain the given text coordinate and provide a border of at least the boundary pixel value. The border cannot always be exact because of the difference between text coordinates and byte-at-a-time window coordinates on some machines.

The four functions are:

```
TextLeft(TX,Boundary:integer):integer;
```

> Returns *X* window coordinate that is at least *Boundary* pixels to the left of the left edge of text coordinate *TX*.

```
TextRight(TX,Boundary:integer):integer;
```

> Returns *X* window coordinate that is at least *Boundary* pixels to the right of the right edge of text coordinate *TX*.

```
TextUp(TY,Boundary:integer):integer;
```

> Returns *Y* window coordinate that is at least *Boundary* pixels above the top edge of text coordinate *TY*.

```
TextDown(TY,Boundary:integer):integer;
```

> Returns *Y* window coordinate that is at least *Boundary* pixels below the bottom edge of text coordinate *TX*.

There are two functions for each direction because the font size is not known to the user program, so the addition of the actual width of the character to its upper lefthand corner coordinate must be done by the system.

Returning to the original example, to define that window enclosing text coordinates [10,2] through [20,4] and give a border of at least 1 pixel on all sides, we use

```
DefineWindow(1,TextLeft(10,1),TextUp(2,1),TextRight(20,1),TextDown(4,1));
```

In addition to the four functions, the procedure

```
DefineTextWindow(I,Left,Up,Right,Down,Border:integer);
```

can also be used to adjust a window to text coordinates. This procedure is a more convenient way to solve the alignment problem, since all parameters are defined in one routine; however, it is less flexible, since the size of the border between text and window boundaries must be the same for all four directions.

Color

The color capabilities of the various Turbo Graphix Toolbox versions range from absolute monochrome (black and white only) to a choice of 16 colors each for the foreground and background. It is very difficult to use the color capabilities in a machine-independent way. The range of colors available is known to the user program, but the actual colors associated with the numbers are not. If two different colors are arbitrarily chosen for foreground and background, there is no way to ensure against, for instance, the choice of blue for foreground and aquamarine for background!

In addition, the consequences of changing the current color vary from machine to machine. On some machines, there may be a considerable delay while pixel colors are being changed. On others, the color may be changed by simply reprogramming the display controller to interpret the same bit patterns as different colors.

Also, on some machines, changing both foreground and background to the same color may destroy the graphic image currently being displayed.

Because of these considerations, it is recommended that programs that are to be used with several versions of the Turbo Graphix Toolbox be written for true black and white.

Speed

The speed of the Turbo Graphix Toolbox varies widely on different machines. The variance is not simple; from one machine to the next, one operation may be twice as fast, and another be about the same speed. You should therefore make no assumptions about speed or timing when you are writing a program that is to run on several machines.

Premature Termination

On some machines, if a program ends while still in graphics mode, the computer may behave erratically. For instance, if a program written for the Hercules graphics card version ends without a call to *LeaveGraphic*, DOS does not know that the screen is in graphics mode, and acts as if it is in text mode.

Included on the Turbo Graphix Toolbox distribution disk is a program, HFIX.COM, to be used to reorient your system after a program terminates improperly. You are free to distribute HFIX.COM with any program you write.

Notes:

Appendix B.
GLOSSARY

absolute screen coordinate system: Coordinate system that uses the entire screen area to plot the pixel location of text or graphics; coordinate [0,0] is in the upper left corner of the screen.

absolute value: The value of a positive or negative number when the sign has been removed. For example, the absolute value of both -2 and $+2$ is 2.

active window: The displayed or RAM (virtual) window in which drawing is currently taking place.

active screen: The displayed or virtual screen in which drawing is currently taking place.

aspect ratio: The horizontal-to-vertical ratio of a circle or ellipse. Used by the Turbo Graphix Toolbox to proportion circles and pie charts.

background: The screen surface and color on which drawing is taking place. See *foreground*.

bar chart: A graph consisting of vertical or horizontal bars with lengths proportioned according to specified quantities.

base point: Any of the points that constitute a graph or curve.

Bezier function: Function that uses an array of control points to construct a parametric, polynomial curve of a predetermined shape.

Cartesian coordinate system: A method used to plot an object's location according to its horizontal-by-vertical position. This position is referenced to horizontal (*X*) and vertical (*Y*) axes.

clipping: Turbo Graphix Toolbox function that keeps graphic images within window or screen boundaries by preventing any part of the drawing that falls outside the window or screen from being displayed.

control point: Any of the points used to plot a graph. Used by the Turbo Graphix Toolbox to construct curves.

coordinate system: A method used to plot an object's location according to its horizontal-by-vertical position. See *absolute screen coordinate system* and *world coordinate system*.

displayed screen: The visible screen displayed on your computer monitor. See *RAM screen*.

flow chart: A graphic representation of a sequence of consecutive events or operations. The Turbo Graphix Toolbox uses a sequence of moving windows to represent a flow chart.

font: Either of two sets of characters used by the Turbo Graphix Toolbox. Window headers, and text that must be in multiples of 4x6 pixels, are displayed in the standard 4x6-pixel text font. All other text is displayed in a machine-dependent, higher resolution text font—8x8-pixels for the IBM card, 9x14 pixels for the Hercules card, and 8x9 pixels for the Zenith card.

foreground: The color used to display text and draw graphic images. See *background*.

graphics mode: Mode of computer operation in which graphics symbols and drawings are displayed. See *text mode*.

header: A user-defined text label, displayed in the Turbo Graphix standard 4x6-pixel font, that is placed either at the top or bottom edge of a window.

histogram: A graphic representation of a frequency distribution that takes the form of a bar chart.

inactive screen: The RAM or displayed screen that is not currently being used for drawing.

include directive: Program comment of the form {*$I filename.ext*} that instructs the compiler to read the program contained in *filename*.

interpolation: Method of determining the value of a function that is between known values, using a procedure or algorithm. See *spline function*.

machine-dependent text: Text that corresponds to the font used by the particular graphics card installed in your system. Text is 8x8-pixels for the IBM card, 8x9 pixels for the Zenith card, and 9x14-pixels for the Hercules card. Machine-dependent text is of a higher resolution than the standard, 4x6-pixel text used by the Turbo Graphix Toolbox to display window headers. See *font*.

modeling: Method used to find the points (and the corresponding function) that will represent a predetermined line, curve, or solid shape. See *Bezier function*.

origin: In any coordinate system, point [0,0], i.e. the point where the coordinate axes intersect.

pie chart: A circular chart used to represent the relative sizes of several quantities that make up a whole unit. The pie chart is divided into sections by radial lines, with each section proportional in angle and area to the quantity it represents.

pixels: Acronym for *picture elements*. The tiny dots that together make up a graphics or text screen display. Pixels are the basic units of measure used by coordinate systems to plot the location of screen objects.

polar coordinate system: Method used to plot a pie chart in reference to its radius and the angle of its first segment.

polygon: A figure that encloses a collection of points, possibly (but not necessarily) connected by line segments.

RAM (virtual) screen: A screen that is stored in RAM memory. It is identical in size and shape to the displayed screen, but any drawing that takes place on it is invisible.

resolution: The quality and accuracy of detail of a displayed image. Resolution depends on the number of pixels within a given area of the screen; the more pixels there are, the higher the resolution.

scaling: Ability of the Turbo Graphix Toolbox to reduce or enlarge an image to fit in a given window according to the world coordinate system specified by the user.

screen coordinate system: See *absolute screen coordinate system*.

spline function: Polynomial function that smooths a curve by calculating and generating additional base points.

step: The increment by which a text character, window, or graphic image moves at one time.

text mode: Computer mode in which only characters are manipulated and displayed. See *graphics mode*.

vertex: The point where the sides of an angle intersect.

virtual screen: See *RAM screen*.

window: An area of the screen specified by the user for drawing. It can range in size between 1 vertical pixel by 8 horizontal pixels and the entire screen.

window definition coordinates: The two sets of X and Y coordinates that define the upper left and lower right corners of a window. Windows are defined on 8-bit horizontal by 1-bit vertical boundaries, so that each X window definition coordinate represents one 8-pixel horizontal unit, and each Y coordinate represents one 1-pixel vertical unit.

window stack: RAM area in which windows can be temporarily stored.

world coordinate system: A user-defined coordinate system that is used to scale drawings within a given window. World X (horizontal) and Y (vertical) coordinates do not necessarily correspond to actual pixel locations, but can be assigned any values that suit the application. A world is enclosed by the X (horizontal) and Y (vertical) coordinates of the upper left and lower right corners of the drawing area.

zero axes: The horizontal (X) and vertical (Y) axes used to plot the location of a screen object.

SUBJECT INDEX

Borland
Software

BORLAND
I N T E R N A T I O N A L   4585 Scotts Valley Drive, Scotts Valley, CA 95066

The ultimate Pascal development environment

Borland's new Turbo Pascal for the Mac™ is so incredibly fast that it can compile 1,420 lines of source code in the 7.1 seconds it took you to read this!

And reading the rest of this takes about *5 minutes*, which is plenty of time for Turbo Pascal for the Mac to compile at least *60,000 more lines* of source code!

Turbo Pascal for the Mac does both Windows and "Units"
The *separate* compilation of routines offered by Turbo Pascal for the Mac creates modules called "Units," which can be linked to any Turbo Pascal® program. This "modular pathway" gives you "pieces" which can then be integrated into larger programs. You get a more efficient use of memory and a reduction in the time it takes to develop large programs.

Turbo Pascal for the Mac is so compatible with Lisa® that they should be living together
Routines from Macintosh Programmer's Workshop Pascal and Inside Macintosh can be compiled and run with only the subtlest changes. Turbo Pascal for the Mac is also compatible with the Hierarchical File System of the Macintosh.™

The 27-second Guide to Turbo Pascal for the Mac

- Compilation speed of more than 12,000 lines per minute
- "Unit" structure lets you create programs in modular form
- Multiple editing windows—up to 8 at once
- Compilation options include compiling to disk or memory, or compile and run
- No need to switch between programs to compile or run a program
- Streamlined development and debugging
- Compatibility with Macintosh Programmer's Workshop Pascal (with minimal changes)
- Compatibility with Hierarchical File System of your Mac
- Ability to define default volume and folder names used in compiler directives
- Search and change features in the editor speed up and simplify alteration of routines
- Ability to use all available Macintosh memory without limit
- "Units" included to call all the routines provided by Macintosh Toolbox

---

3 MacWinners from Borland!
First there was SideKick for the Mac,™ then Reflex for the Mac,™ and now Turbo Pascal for the Mac™!

Suggested Retail Price: $99.95 (not copy protected)

Minimum system configuration:
256K. One 400K drive.

BORLAND
I N T E R N A T I O N A L

TURBO PASCAL
TURBO TUTOR®

VERSION 2.0

Learn Pascal From The Folks Who Created The Turbo Pascal® Family

Borland International proudly presents Turbo Tutor, the perfect complement to your Turbo Pascal compiler. Turbo Tutor is really for everyone— even if you've never programmed before.

And if you're already proficient, Turbo Tutor can sharpen up the fine points. The manual and program disk focus on the whole spectrum of Turbo Pascal programming techniques.

- **For the Novice:** It gives you a concise history of Pascal, tells you how to write a simple program, and defines the basic programming terms you need to know.

- **Programmer's Guide:** The heart of Turbo Pascal. The manual covers the fine points of every aspect of Turbo Pascal programming: program structure, data types, control structures, procedures and functions, scalar types, arrays, strings, pointers, sets, files, and records.

- **Advanced Concepts:** If you're an expert, you'll love the sections detailing such topics as linked lists, trees, and graphs. You'll also find sample program examples for PC-DOS and MS-DOS.®

10,000 lines of commented source code, demonstrations of 20 Turbo Pascal features, multiple-choice quizzes, an interactive on-line tutor, and more!

Turbo Tutor may be the only reference work about Pascal and programming you'll ever need!

Suggested Retail Price: $39.95 (not copy protected)

Minimum system configuration: Turbo Pascal 3.0. PC-DOS (MS-DOS) 2.0 or later. 192K RAM minimum (CP/M-80 version 2.2 or later: 64K RAM minimum).

BORLAND
INTERNATIONAL

Turbo Pascal and Turbo Tutor are registered trademarks of Borland International Inc. CP/M is a registered trademark of Digital Research Inc. MS-DOS is a registered trademark of Microsoft Corp.   BOR 0064B

TURBO PASCAL GAMEWORKS®

Secrets And Strategies Of The Masters Are Revealed For The First Time

Explore the world of state-of-the-art computer games with Turbo GameWorks. Using easy-to-understand examples, Turbo GameWorks teaches you techniques to quickly create your own computer games using Turbo Pascal.® Or, for instant excitement, play the three great computer games we've included on disk—compiled and ready to run.

TURBO CHESS

Test your chess-playing skills against your computer challenger. With Turbo GameWorks, you're on your way to becoming a master chess player. Explore the complete Turbo Pascal source code and discover the secrets of Turbo Chess.

"What impressed me the most was the fact that with this program you can become a computer chess analyst. You can add new variations to the program at any time and make the program play stronger and stronger chess. There's no limit to the fun and enjoyment of playing Turbo GameWorks Chess, and most important of all, with this chess program there's no limit to how it can help you improve your game."

—George Koltanowski, Dean of American Chess, former President of the United Chess Federation, and syndicated chess columnist.

TURBO BRIDGE

Now play the world's most popular card game—bridge. Play one-on-one with your computer or against up to three other opponents. With Turbo Pascal source code, you can even program your own bidding or scoring conventions.

"There has never been a bridge program written which plays at the expert level, and the ambitious user will enjoy tackling that challenge, with the format already structured in the program. And for the inexperienced player, the bridge program provides an easy-to-follow format that allows the user to start right out playing. The user can 'play bridge' against real competition without having to gather three other people."

—Kit Woolsey, writer of several articles and books on bridge, and twice champion of the Blue Ribbon Pairs.

TURBO GO-MOKU

Prepare for battle when you challenge your computer to a game of Go-Moku—the exciting strategy game also known as Pente.® In this battle of wits, you and the computer take turns placing X's and O's on a grid of 19×19 squares until five pieces are lined up in a row. Vary the game if you like, using the source code available on your disk.

Suggested Retail Price: $69.95 (not copy protected)

Minimum system configuration: IBM PC, XT, AT, Portable, 3270, PCjr, and true compatibles. PC-DOS (MS-DOS) 2.0 or later. 192K RAM minimum. To edit and compile the Turbo Pascal source code, you must be using Turbo Pascal 3.0 for IBM PCs and compatibles.

 **BORLAND** *INTERNATIONAL*

Turbo Pascal and Turbo GameWorks are registered trademarks of Borland International, Inc. Pente is a registered trademark of Parker Brothers. IBM, XT, AT, and PCjr are registered trademarks of International Business Machines Corporation. MS-DOS is a registered trademark of Microsoft Corporation.

BOR 0065B

LIGHTNING WORD WIZARD™

Lightning Word Wizard includes complete, commented Turbo Pascal® source code and all the technical information you'll need to understand and work with Turbo Lightning's "engine." More than 20 fully documented Turbo Pascal procedures reveal powerful Turbo Lightning engine calls. Harness the full power of the complete and authoritative Random House® Concise Word List and Random House Thesaurus.

Turbo Lightning's "Reference Manual"

Developers can use the versatile on-line examples to harness Turbo Lightning's power to do rapid word searches. Lightning Word Wizard is the forerunner of the database access systems that will incorporate and engineer the Turbo Lightning Library™ of electronic reference works.

The ultimate collection of word games and crossword solvers!

The excitement, challenge, competition, and education of four games and three solver utilities—puzzles, scrambles, spell-searches, synonym-seekings, hidden words, crossword solutions, and more. You and your friends (up to four people total) can set the difficulty level and contest the high-speed smarts of Lightning Word Wizard!

Turbo Lightning—Critics' Choice

"Lightning's good enough to make programmers and users cheer, executives of other software companies weep." **Jim Seymour, *PC Week***

"The real future of Lightning clearly lies not with the spelling checker and thesaurus currently included, but with other uses of its powerful look-up engine." **Ted Silveira, *Profiles***

"This newest product from Borland has it all." **Don Roy, *Computing Now!***

Minimum system configuration: IBM PC, XT, AT, PCjr, Portable, and true compatibles. 256K RAM minimum. PC-DOS (MS-DOS) 2.0 or greater. Turbo Lightning software required. Optional—Turbo Pascal 3.0 or greater to edit and compile Turbo Pascal source code.

BORLAND INTERNATIONAL

Suggested Retail Price: $69.95
(not copy protected)

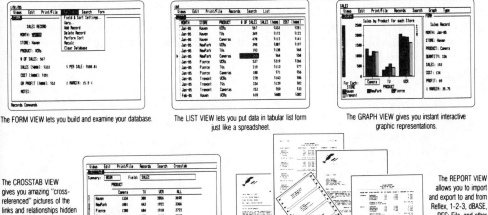
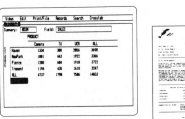

REFLEX WORKSHOP™

Includes 22 "instant templates" covering a broad range of business applications (listed below). Also shows you how to customize databases, graphs, crosstabs, and reports. It's an invaluable analytical tool and an important addition to another one of our best sellers, Reflex: The Analyst 1.1.

Fast-start tutorial examples:

Learn Reflex® as you work with practical business applications. The Reflex Workshop Disk supplies databases and reports large enough to illustrate the power and variety of Reflex features. Instructions in each Reflex Workshop chapter take you through a step-by-step analysis of sample data. You then follow simple steps to adapt the files to your own needs.

22 practical business applications:

Workshop's 22 "instant templates" give you a wide range of analytical tools:

Administration
- Scheduling Appointments
- Planning Conference Facilities
- Managing a Project
- Creating a Mailing System
- Managing Employment Applications

Sales and Marketing
- Researching Store Check Inventory
- Tracking Sales Leads
- Summarizing Sales Trends
- Analyzing Trends

Production and Operations
- Summarizing Repair Turnaround

- Tracking Manufacturing Quality Assurance
- Analyzing Product Costs

Accounting and Financial Planning
- Tracking Petty Cash
- Entering Purchase Orders
- Organizing Outgoing Purchase Orders
- Analyzing Accounts Receivable
- Maintaining Letters of Credit
- Reporting Business Expenses
- Managing Debits and Credits
- Examining Leased Inventory Trends
- Tracking Fixed Assets
- Planning Commercial Real Estate Investment

Whether you're a newcomer learning Reflex basics or an experienced "power user" looking for tips, Reflex Workshop will help you quickly become an expert database analyst.

Minimum system configuration: IBM PC, AT, and XT, and true compatibles. PC-DOS (MS-DOS) 2.0 or greater. 384K RAM minimum. Requires Reflex: The Analyst, and IBM Color Graphics Adapter, Hercules Monochrome Graphics Card or equivalent.

BORLAND
INTERNATIONAL

Suggested Retail Price: $69.95
(not copy protected)

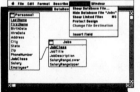
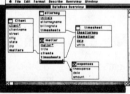

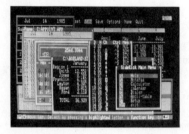
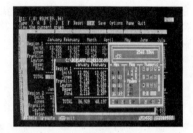

Traveling SIDEKICK®

The Organizer For The Computer Age!

Traveling SideKick is *BinderWare*,™ both a binder you take with you when you travel and a software program—which includes a Report Generator—that *generates* and *prints out* all the information you'll need to take with you.

Information like your phone list, your client list, your address book, your calendar, and your appointments. The appointment or calendar files you're already using in your SideKick® can automatically be used by your Traveling SideKick. You don't waste time and effort reentering information that's already there.

One keystroke prints out a form like your address book. No need to change printer paper;

you simply punch three holes, fold and clip the form into your Traveling SideKick binder, and you're on your way. Because Traveling SideKick is CAD (Computer-Age Designed), you don't fool around with low-tech tools like scissors, tape, or staples. And because Traveling SideKick is electronic, it works this year, next year, and all the "next years" after that. Old-fashioned daytime organizers are history in 365 days.

What's inside Traveling SideKick

TABLET OF EXTRA FORMS
IN POCKET ON BACK FLAP, FOR USE IN ANY OF THE ORGANIZER SECTIONS.

ADDRESS BOOK SECTION
PREPRINTED ADDRESS FORMS WITH TABBED DIVIDERS FOR EASY REFERENCE.

MISCELLANEOUS SECTION
TO STORE ALL EXTRA PREPRINTED FORMS AND COMMONLY-USED RECORDS.

ROLLER BALLPOINT PEN
BLACK PEN THAT FITS IN FLAP FOR EASY ACCESS.

REFERENCE SECTION
CONTAINS MAPS THAT SHOW AREA CODES AND TIME ZONES, TOLL-FREE NUMBERS FOR TRAVEL ACCOMODATIONS, METRIC CONVERSION CHARTS.

FINANCE SECTION
MULTI-USE LEDGER FORMS, RECEIPT LOG AND STORAGE ENVELOPE, CREDIT CARD INFORMATION.

CALENDAR SECTION
YEARLY, MONTHLY, WEEKLY, AND DAILY ENGAGEMENT CALENDARS SUPPLEMENT THOSE YOU PRINT OUT WITH TRAVELING SIDEKICK

PENDING SECTION
A "TO BE CONTINUED" SECTION FOR CURRENT PROJECTS, MEETING NOTES, ETC.

CALCULATOR
IN ONE OF TWO BUSINESS-CARD-SIZE STORAGE POCKETS.

TRAVELING SIDEKICK SOFTWARE
GENERATES, UPDATES, AND PRINTS YOUR ADDRESS AND CALENDAR FILES.

What the software program and its Report Generator do for you before you go—and when you get back

Before you go:
- Prints out your calendar, appointments, addresses, phone directory, and whatever other information you need from your data files

When you return:
- Lets you quickly and easily enter all the new names you obtained while you were away into your SideKick data files

It can also:
- Sort your address book by contact, zip code or company name
- Print mailing labels
- Print information selectively
- Search files for existing addresses or calendar engagements

***Suggested Retail Price: $69.95**

Minimum system configuration: IBM PC, XT, AT, Portable, PCjr, 3270 and true compatibles. PC-DOS (MS-DOS) 2.0 or later. 256K RAM mimimum.

*Special introductory offer

BORLAND
INTERNATIONAL

SideKick and Traveling SideKick are registered trademarks and BinderWare is a trademark of Borland International, Inc. IBM, AT, XT, and PCjr are registered trademarks of International Business Machines Corp. MS-DOS is a registered trademark of Microsoft Corp. BOR 0083

SuperKey®

Increased Productivity for Anyone Using IBM®PCs or Compatibles

SuperKey turns 1,000 keystrokes into 1!

Yes, SuperKey can *record* lengthy keystroke sequences and play them back at the touch of a single key. Instantly. Like magic.

Say, for example, you want to add a column of figures in 1-2-3.® Without SuperKey, you'd have to type 5 keystrokes just to get started: @ s u m (. With SuperKey, you can turn those 5 keystrokes into 1.

SuperKey keeps your confidential files—CONFIDENTIAL!

Time after time you've experienced it: anyone can walk up to your PC and read your confidential files (tax returns, business plans, customer lists, personal letters, etc.).

With SuperKey you can encrypt any file, even while running another program. As long as you keep the password secret, only YOU can decode your file correctly. SuperKey also implements the U.S. government Data Encryption Standard (DES).

SuperKey helps protect your capital investment

SuperKey, at your convenience, will make your screen go blank after a predetermined time of screen/keyboard inactivity. You've paid hard-earned money for your PC. SuperKey will protect your monitor's precious phosphor and your investment.

SuperKey protects your work from intruders while you take a break

Now you can lock your keyboard at any time. Prevent anyone from changing hours of work. Type in your secret password and everything comes back to life—just as you left it.

Suggested Retail Price: $69.95 (not copy protected)

Minimum system configuration: IBM PC, XT, AT, PCjr, and true compatibles. PC-DOS (MS-DOS) 2.0 or greater. 128K RAM.
One disk drive.

BORLAND
INTERNATIONAL

SuperKey is a registered trademark of Borland International, Inc. IBM, XT, AT,
and PCjr are registered trademarks of International Business Machines Corp. 1-2-3 is a
registered trademark of Lotus Development Corp. MS-DOS is a registered trademark of
Microsoft Corp.

BOR 0062B

How To Buy Borland Software

BORLAND
INTERNATIONAL

NOT COPY PROTECTED

To Order By Credit Card, Call **(800) 255-8008**

60 DAY MONEY-BACK GUARANTEE

In California call **(800) 742-1133**